Write Nonfiction NOW!

GUIDE TO
WRITING
A
BOOK
IN
30 DAYS

Revised and Expanded

NINA AMIR

PURE SPIRIT
CREATIONS

Published 2024 by Pure Spirit Creations

www.purespiritcreations.com
Placitas, NM

Ordering Information:
Special discounts are available on quantity purchases
by corporations, associations, and others.
For details, contact nina@ninaamir.com.

Layout and Design by Shabbir Hussain Badshah.

Cover Design by Daniel Eyenegho.

Author photo by Rick Rood.

The Write Nonfiction NOW!
Guide to Writing a Book in 30 Days
Revised and Expanded/Nina Amir—3rd ed.

ISBN (paperback): 978-0-9835353-7-9

Table of Contents

INTRODUCTION

Taking on the
Book-in-a-Month Challenge

By Nina Amir

Y ou want to write a book in a month.

Eighty-one percent of the U.S. population says they want to write a book, but most remain wannabe authors. In fact, only about two percent ever write and publish a book.

Yet, you want to accomplish this feat in 30 days. Good for you!

My desire is for you to join the two percent and transform yourself from aspiring to published author. One of the best ways to accomplish this goal is to take on a write-a-book-in-a-month challenge. That's why I created the Write Nonfiction in November Challenge (WNFIN), also known as National Nonfiction Writing Month (NaNonFiWriMo).

However, you don't have to wait until November to write a nonfiction book in a month. You can do it at any time, and I encourage you to start now!

Before you can take on any challenge, though, you must be prepared. In this case, you have to know how to write a marketable book quickly, effectively, and with a fair degree of craft. Additionally, you need the knowledge, experience, and information to fill the pages of your manuscript.

I created this first book in *The Write Nonfiction NOW! Guide* series to help you prepare to do just that. Much of the information is culled from past WNFIN events, which annually offered 30 blog post from guest experts on the topics of writing, publishing, promoting, and building a business around nonfiction. In addition, the first and second editions included some never-before-seen material. The third edition features seven new chapters related to writing a book in a month, all of which appeared on my blog, Write Nonfiction NOW!, since the first edition was released in 2014. Plus, I have revised and expanded some of the existing chapters. The vast amount of information and expertise represented by the 11 authors in this resource provides you with a comprehensive guide to starting and finishing any type of nonfiction book in a month.

Don't wait any longer. Read on, set your deadline, and then write your nonfiction book in 30 days! Take that first step and leave the ranks of wannabe authors behind. One month from now, you will have created the first draft of your book and be well on the way to transforming yourself into a nonfiction author.

Get It Done

Why would anyone want to write a nonfiction book in a month? To get the project done, that's why.

You also may want to push yourself to do more, perform at a higher level, or fulfill your potential. Or you chose to take on a book-in-a-month challenge in an effort to develop greater productivity, stop procrastinating, and commit to your writing. It's also possible that you decided to join a 30-day writing event to develop a consistent writing habit.

You may have lots of nonfiction book ideas (or just one) in your head that you haven't gotten down on paper, published, and into the hands of readers. It's easy to claim you don't have time to write because you are too busy with work, family, or life in general. These excuses keep the books stuck in your head.

A 30-day writing challenge helps you carve out time to write.

You already realize that you won't make the positive and meaningful impact on readers you could if you don't write and publish your brilliant book ideas. Not only that, but you also won't fulfill your potential or your purpose in life.

That's where a month-long writing challenge proves helpful and truly important in your life. It forces you to get an amazing amount of work done in a short period of time. It gives you a reason to get that book out of your head—to tell your story, offer your wisdom or information, or use your expertise or experience—in just 30 days. It provides you with the opportunity to become the person you know you are or can be—a nonfiction author—and to serve others in the process.

A Deadline Is a Writer's Best Friend

I'm a magazine journalist by trade and education; I know the value of deadlines. Some people hate them, but I call them my "friends." They help me get my work done and make me do so fast! And when I've met a deadline, I get to check that item off my to-do list. I get the satisfaction of knowing I've accomplished my goal. Not only that, if it's a goal that has personal significance to me, I am left feeling as if I've reached a higher level of performance and possibly made a difference in the world.

That's why I love a writing challenge. It's a deadline you set to help you reach a professional or personal goal. It's not a contest. It's an opportunity you create for yourself to do what you want to do in a specific amount of time. With a book-in-a-month challenge, you start and complete a nonfiction book in 30 days—because you set that deadline. You accept the opportunity. The prize is the manuscript in your hand and how great you feel about yourself for achieving your goal. Additionally, you transform in the process or writing the book, and you pay that forward by providing readers with the chance to transform once they get the book in their hands.

At the very least, at the end of a month-long nonfiction book writing challenge you can mark "Write my book" off your to-do list. How great is that? You'll have a manuscript (or possibly even a published e-book) ready to be polished up for publication. And you'll be one gigantic step closer to realizing your goal, fulfilling your potential, and providing readers with a book that could change their lives.

Generate Time and Energy

If you are afraid that you don't have what it takes to meet a book-in-a month challenge, don't worry. The biggest step is making the decision. Once you've done that, you rise to the occasion. You discover that you suddenly have more commitment, energy, time, and passion for your project. You won't have to power through your daily writing goals; it will be easy! You'll have set your intention, and you'll be focused and on purpose.

Deciding to take a challenge helps you generate the time and energy you need to complete it. Once the decision is made, you become inspired. You spot holes in your schedule, or create them, so you can meet your deadline. The fact that you've made the commitment is exciting! That, in and of itself, raises your energy and gives you more focus. Both help you get your book written fast.

Fitting a Writing Challenge into Your Life

That's not to say that life might not get in the way—if you let it. That's part of the challenge. If you set up your days so you "make time" for your book project, you'll see that it's possible to write almost every day *no matter what*. And it's possible to make up for lost time on other days—all because you know you have a deadline and you're committed to meeting it.

You do, however, have to schedule time for this book-in-a-month challenge. That starts with clarity about your book. Determine the approximate length of your book; then you can do the math and figure out how many words you need to write per day. A 50,000-word manuscript requires a commitment to write 1,667 words per day every single day of the week. You probably don't want to write a book that is much longer than that . . . at least not in a month. Most memoirs, however, are quite a bit longer, so remember that if you plan to tackle your life story in 30 days.

With this information in mind, look at your life—specifically your calendar. The only way your book will get written in a month is if you schedule in writing time. (It helps to know how fast you write. I can churn out about 1,000 words in an hour, for example, if I don't need to call on research—and don't research while you write!) It's great if you can write six days per week so you have some time off to rejuvenate and stay inspired. You also can use the seventh day as a make-up day. If you don't meet your word quota for the week, you must write on the seventh day; if you do meet your quota, it's a free day.

Once you've scheduled the days on your calendar, be certain you have enough writing sessions to complete your book in a month. Calculate the number of sessions and multiply this by the number of words you think you can produce in each session (given the length of the session); it should equal the number of words in your final manuscript or come close (your word count may change when you revise). Add in a few extra "emergency" sessions because life happens, especially at the most inopportune times.

A Challenge All Year Long

When the 30-day challenge is over and you write "The End," here's what you will have learned: You can write a nonfiction book, and you can do it in 30 days. Not only that, you can do it again—any time you choose.

That's a huge discovery if you have a lot of book ideas in your head that you want to get out. Just give yourself a 30-day challenge at any time of the year—maybe schedule one book-in-a-month challenge every quarter of the year, and you're off and writing. You don't need to wait for National Nonfiction Writing Month or any other book-in-a-month event. Just write when you want to get a nonfiction book idea out of your head and onto the page.

Using this strategy increases your productivity tremendously. Imagine the catalog of works you'd amass if you wrote a book in a month twice a year or four times a year . . .

When I wrote, *The Author Training Manual: Develop Marketable Ideas, Craft Books That Sell, Become the Author Publishers Want, and Self-Publish Effectively*, I completed the first draft in six weeks. No, not quite a month, but close. You can see how training yourself to write books fast—in a month—can change your status as a writer. You'll become not just an author but a multiple-book author quickly.

I encourage you not to think of your book-in-a-month challenge as a one-time event. Think of it as a regular activity. Therein lies the real challenge if you want to become a high-performance and highly productive nonfiction author.

Can You Write a *Good* Book in a Month

There are plenty of challenges, courses, and programs meant to encourage you to write a book in a month. Yet, many people balk at this idea because they believe it takes a long time to write a book. That explains why I'm often asked if it's possible to write a book, or a *good book*, in a just 30 days.

My short answer is: Yes. Of course, you can write a good book in 30 days.

I know plenty of nonfiction writers who write a draft in 30 days, and those first drafts are not shitty, schlock, or dreck or any other name you want to assign to something you'd put in the circular file (the trash can).

It's also possible to turn out an entire finished manuscript in 30 days. There are instances when a writer sits down, and a book simply flows out of them start to finish in record time. They may feel so inspired they don't sleep much, and they eat at their computer and only stop writing when "nature calls." Such writers may produce a manuscript that needs little to no editing and do so in just a matter of a few weeks. Then, they send it off to an editor who returns it in also in just a few weeks, and, voilà, the work is ready for publication.

In most cases, to finish a polished manuscript in a month means tackling a shorter book. To publish it as well in that amount of time you might also want to take on a short project. (<u>Learn more about writing a short book fast here</u> and in a forthcoming chapter.)

It's also possible to turn out a good book in a month by using repurposed material—at least in part. You may have essays, articles or blog posts that can be compiled and revised or edited into a book in little time. Most likely you will need to add content to produce a good book from repurposed material, but you can do this quickly. (Learn more about that in my book, *How to Blog a Book*.) Keep in mind that the eBook you are reading consists primarily of repurposed material, specifically blog posts.

Many book-in-a-month challenges can be completed with repurposed content if they don't "require" previously unpublished material. If the content you produced previously was good, you will produce a good book.

Although many writers who produce good books in a month are practiced at writing books, that doesn't preclude you from following in their footsteps if you are a newbie writer. Really, all you need to accomplish this goal is:

- **An idea**: You must start with an idea. You can't flounder around wondering what to write about for the first week.

- **The commitment**: You must be committed to writing a book in a month. And no matter what challenges come up during those 30 days, your commitment must be strong enough to push you forward to meet your goal. You must have the determination to put your butt in the chair every day for a month and churn out words.

- **A plan**: The more planning you do before the month begins, the easier it will be for you to meet your goal by month's end. This is true not only for your book project but for your personal calendar. Be sure you know what you will write, how you will write it and what resources or research you need to write your book as well as how much time it will require and how you will fit this time into your daily calendar.

- **The mindset:** If you believe it will take a long time to write a book or a good book, that's the reality you create. If your thoughts are focused on "Books take a long time to write," "Writing a book is hard," "Writing a good book is supposed to take at least a year," or anything along these lines, that is exactly what the experience becomes for you, and you won't be able to write a book in a month. You must have the mindset, the belief system or thoughts, that allow you to write a book in a month.

- **The Identity:** Mindset and habits flow out of identity or who you believe you are. If you believe, "I am someone who can't write a book in a month," you will struggle to do so. Decide "I am someone who easily writes books in a month," and the challenge will be easy. Why? You will BE the type of person who has the mindset and habits that allow you to take the necessary actions to reach that goal.

Keep in mind that "good" is a subjective term. Your interpretation of what constitutes a good book might be different from what a literary agent, publishing house acquisitions editor, or your mother deem a good book.

The Starting Point

No matter where you are in the process of becoming a nonfiction author, it's time to start your book. Make the decision, then take action. And stay committed to your goal and your new identity. These are the ways your book will get written in a month.

The primary things to remember are:

- **Prepare.** Take the time before you begin to ideate your book's content and to give it a structure. You don't want to stare at a blank screen but rather to know what content you need to produce. This helps you write fast and with confidence.

- **Make space and time.** Put "writing" on your schedule each day and create a distraction-free zone to get your daily word quota done. This is how you will meet your goals.

- **Stick to your commitment.** Be accountable to yourself—or be accountable to someone else. Don't let yourself off the hook. Have self-integrity. No excuses; the book *must* be done by the end of the month, even if that means sacrificing television time, reading for pleasure, that extra tap of the snooze button, or something else you enjoy.

- **Have a successful Author Attitude.** Attitude plays such a huge role in meeting any challenge. Check in with yourself before you start your book-in-a-month challenge. Are you willing to do what it takes? Are you feeling positive and confident? If not, it's time to work on your attitude, and to develop some strong affirmations to help you change your outlook to one that reinforces a sense of "I can do it" and "I'm good enough" every day and each time you sit down to write. (Such "I AM" statements develop the identity you need to succeed at the writing challenge.) Do not get stuck in the victim mentality of "Life always gets in the way." Instead, tell yourself, "I am someone who always finds a way to get my writing done because it's my priority and I am committed to this activity." Be a writer who gets from the first word of your manuscript to "The End."

You will find information on all these areas in the following sections of this book. Once you have these things in place, you're ready to start your book-in-a-month challenge.

PREPARATION

How to Prepare for a 30-Day Writing Challenge

By Nina Amir

I hope you have decided to take the <u>Write Nonfiction in November Challenge</u> and join in the excitement created by so many writers around the world attempting to write a book in 30 days. (If you write fiction, you can check out <u>National Novel Writing Month</u>.) When you set a goal to start and finish a work of nonfiction in a month, whether it's a full-length book, a short eBook, an article, an essay, or some sort of report or proposal, preparation helps you achieve success. So, today I want to discuss a few types of preparation you might undertake.

As with any activity that requires extreme amounts of energy, focus and productivity for a short period, you must get ready. Compare writing a book in a month to running a marathon. You can't just run a marathon without training before the big day. Book-in-a-month events writing marathons. That's why you have to spend time preparing before the challenge begins, and the preparation ensures you cross the finish line with a manuscript in hand.

Don't make the mistake of ignoring preparation . . . if you want to finish a book in 30 days. The writers who decide to write a book in a month but fail to do so have one thing in common—lack of preparation. Don't follow in their footsteps. Take the time to do the preparation necessary so you succeed at completing your nonfiction book manuscript in a month.

With that in mind, here are suggested ways to prepare for a 30-day writing challenge. Take the time to apply them and you increase your chances of success.

Do your research prior to the start of the event.

Research can slow down your progress during a 30-day writing challenge. During this period, you only want to write.

You know why… You've probably had this experience: You're in the flow, writing productively, and suddenly you realize you need a bit of research. So, you stop writing and click through to the Internet. Or you go to your bookshelf to search for a book you know contains the information you need. Three hours later, you haven't written a word—and *maybe* you found the information you needed.

Don't do this! Instead, do your research before you begin the 30-day writing event. Have all your project research and information close at hand so you don't need to stop and search for it during your writing marathon. Organize your research well so you can easily access whatever you need as you write.

If you discover you need more research while working on your manuscript, don't stop writing; instead place a bracket in your manuscript with the words [add research], and keep writing. Then, when you edit, you'll remember you needed information, and you can find it at that time.

Even better, schedule a research day during or after November. (You can even have one time block for research each week if necessary.) Do a search on your document for the word "research," and start filling in the blanks by addressing each each one individually.

Plan your nonfiction book (or project) in advance.

You can predetermine the structure and content of a nonfiction book before you write it—and you should. <u>That's why you produce a business</u>

plan for a book. When you know how many chapters you need to write and what content each chapter contains, you have a good idea of how long it will take to write each chapter. This information helps you schedule enough writing time on your calendar, so you finish your project in 30-days. Also, you won't spend time staring at a blank screen if you plan out your book's content.

Use a mind map, an outline or bullet points to plan your book's structure or content. For a book, this could be a table of contents, and you can break the table of contents into smaller bits, like subheadings. You could also compose chapter summaries, which are short written synopsis of each chapter.

Brainstorming your content and organizing it in advance allows you to power through your writing periods without wondering what to write. It also helps you write a better first draft because it will need less reorganizing later. Following a writing guide, like a detailed outline, keeps you from going off on tangents or being redundant.

Know how much time you need daily to meet your goal.

One of the most common reason people don't follow through on their plans to write anything tends to be lack of time or "other commitments." Plan your schedule for the next month in advance so you have ample time to meet your 30-day writing goal. Consider what can be put on the back burner for a month, how you will rearrange your life, and in what ways you will make time for this writing challenge.

If you planned out your book, you know approximately how long it will take to complete the manuscript. But if you don't make time to write your book during November—just like at any other time of the year, it won't happen.

Break your estimated project time into daily writing periods or time blocks. If you've estimated that it will take you 30 hours, that's an hour per day. But what if you miss a day? Plan a few longer writing periods on the weekend or add an extra day or two into your writing schedule.

If you are working with a word count, then determine out how many words you need to write per day to meet you goal. To complete a 50,000-word nonfiction book in 30 days requires writing 1,667 words daily. Since you might miss a day or that goal occasionally, add a few extra writing periods to your November calendar as "catch-up" times.

No matter how full your typical weekly schedule, "calendar" your writing periods. Get out your calendar and find times to write—even if they are only 30-minute appointments with yourself. Get them scheduled!

Change your internal dialogue.

Mindset makes a huge difference in whether you achieve any type of goal. Your mindset is reflective of your internal dialogue. This mental chatter consists of your thoughts and beliefs, specifically about your ability to write and complete a book in a month.

Consider if you have self-defeating thoughts, such as:

- "I don't really think I'll complete my project, but I'll see how far I get."

- "I never finish anything I start."

- "I never have enough time for challenges like this."

- "My writing is no good; I don't know why I try."

- "I have nothing to say worth reading."

If your mental chatter includes such statements, now is the time to change your internal dialogue into affirmations, or statements that are more positive and supportive. These might include:

- "I always complete my projects."

- "I finish everything I start."

- "I always have enough time for challenges like this."

- "I'm a good writer."
- "I have something to say that is worth reading."

Thoughts entertained often become beliefs. If you believe you can do something, you will—or you'll find a way. So place your attention on what you can do rather than on what you can't.

Adopt an Author Attitude.

Successful writers have an "Author Attitude," which consists of willingness, optimism, objectivity, and tenacity. You will need all these qualities during a 30-day writing challenge. This attitude ensures you:

- Do whatever it takes to meet your goal.
- See obstacles as challenges and meet them head on.
- Offer encouragement, rather than self-criticism, about your work.
- Act with persistence, determination and perseverance.

To learn more about "Author Attitude," check out my book *The Author Training Manual*, or invest in the <u>Author Training 101-104</u> program.

Have a Version–1.0 attitude.

To produce a first draft of your book in only 30 days, you need a Version–1.0 attitude, not a Version 2.0 or even 3.0 attitude.

During a book-in-a-month challenge, you set out to complete a first draft of your book—not a final, finished manuscript. That's the goal. The draft is the beginning...always. You can edit it, improve it, revise it, or even rewrite it later. But if you don't have a first draft, then... well...you have little to work with.

Leave your Inner Perfectionist at the door each time you sit down to write. Leave your Inner Editor outside as well. Invite your Inner Writer to come along and write...as fast or as steadily as you can.

Create a space conducive to writing.

If you don't have an office or writing desk already, clear a space in your home where you can write. Your writing space should be a sacred place where you go to create your work—in November and beyond. Use it for writing . . . nothing else.

It's difficult to work in a cluttered space, sitting on a bed, or on the couch while your significant other or children watch television. If you have no space in your home, then find a coffee shop you like or a local library. Bring along some comfort or sacred objects.

Also, ensure you have all the necessary writing materials you need close at hand. This includes, of course, your computer—charged, backed up, and ready to go. Also consider if your printer has enough ink in the cartridge, if you need pens or pencils, paper, certain books, a Google Docs folder to save your draft in the cloud, or a binder for your printed pages. You might also want to stock up on your favorite snacks and drinks.

Remove distractions when you write.

Distractions can become the largest obstacle to finish your book draft in 30 days. Take an accounting of what distracts you most or most often. Is it your kids, your pets, social media, texts, phone calls, television, the laundry, or something else. Then, develop strategies for reducing or eliminating these distractions.

For example, noise-canceling headphones work great to cut out the distractions of chatter and music in a public place or even your children arguing or playing a computer game in the next room.

You can get rid of the distractions of email, your phone and social media by turning off the internet, shutting down devices, and quieting email and social media notifications. Or you can opt to use some more drastic measures. Discover a plethora of solutions with a Google search (before November), or read this post, which offers seven ways to block out noise and distraction.

Find a writing buddy or buddies.

Gathering a group of writers who all opted into a month-long writing challenge can prove enormously powerful. All the participants cheer each other on until they reach the finish line. You are all in it together and share the experience as well as the goal.

That's why the National Fiction Writing Month (NaNoWriMo) "write-ins" work. People get together to write. They are accountable to each other. The do writing sprints and compete for the highest word count.

Or find an accountability partner or writing buddy. Such a person should be willing to hold you to your daily or weekly writing goals, not someone who says, "Oh, it's okay that you were too tired today to write. You'll do better tomorrow." You want a buddy who says, "Take a power nap, eat a protein bar, do ten jumping jacks, and then sit down in the chair and write! You can do it! I know you can churn out your word count for today…and I want you to call me or email me when you've done it. NO excuses." This person does not have to be a writer.

Take care of yourself physically.

You can't finish a marathon if you don't, for example, hydrate along the way. The same goes for a writing marathon.

Even though you may squeeze your writing time into an already over-filled schedule, make time to walk, sleep, eat, and drink enough before and during the month. Self-care gives you the energy to make it from Day 1 to Day 30 of the challenge.

Pick a doable project.

Don't try to write a 100,000-word memoir—from first to final draft—in a month. That's crazy. You might write the first draft of a 75,000-word memoir in a month if you have many hours per day to devote to it. (That's about 10 pages per day. How long would it take you to write 10 pages?)

Choose a doable project, like an article or two, four essays, a 5,000- to 30,000-word eBook, or even the first draft of a 50,000 prescriptive nonfiction book. You can reasonably complete these projects in 30 days.

Remember: a 30-day writing event is like a marathon. Prepare. Then write your nonfiction book consistently to cross the finish line in 30 days.

Get Ready to Write a Nonfiction Book in a Month

By Jay Artale

If you want to write a nonfiction book in a month, you can't just turn up on day one and expect to be ready for the challenge. Writing a book in an accelerated timeframe is like running a sprint. You wouldn't show up at the starting line of a race without a period of training and limbering up first, so why would you show up unprepared for a writing sprint?

The lead-up to a 30-day writing event is a training period. Use that time to get yourself in the right head-space and establish habits that will maintain your momentum.

This training period is where you can allow yourself to fail. The only way to find out what daily writing approach works with your daily schedule is through a process of elimination. There's no room in a sprint for trial and error; that's what your training period is for.

When I tried my first National Novel Writing Month event, I was wholly unprepared and gave up on the challenge by the end of the first week. The next year I did a bit of planning but still didn't see the challenge through to the end. Then, I wrote my first draft of a nonfiction book in a month, and I self-published it.

What made the difference? My preparation.

Develop a Writing Habit

To meet your nonfiction writing challenge goals, you must write every day. If you miss a day, that increases the pressure to perform on successive days. For example, if you're planning on writing a 30,000-word first draft within 30 days, your target is 1,000 words a day, but your daily target increases as soon as you miss a day. If you miss too many days, that target will seem unachievable, and you'll give up.

Common wisdom says it takes 21 days to create a new habit. (Some studies say it takes much longer). That means your training period needs to start at least three weeks before you're due to start your writing sprint. You don't have to begin by writing 1,000 words per day—you can work up to it over the training period.

Or just use this time to establish a daily writing habit. Simply, write for the same amount of time every day.

Make Time to Write

During this run-up to your writing sprint, you can write anything. It's not important *what* you write; you must get words onto a page and train your writing muscles to perform consistently. You also want to develop the mindset and identity that you are someone who writes daily.

Discover what time of day you're most productive. Experiment by writing at different times and see which works best for you. I love getting up earlier than usual and starting my day with a writing session. That way, nothing competes for my time, and I'm not trying to juggle other tasks to make room to write.

Before I abandoned my corporate career, I used to write in the cracks of life: a quick writing session before work, half of my lunch hour, stay at work late, squeeze in a writing session while making tea, type on my phone in the coffee or supermarket queue, or swap my gym workout for a power walk around the building while using my voice to text to capture my content.

Discover Your Distractions

It's easy to find an excuse *not* to write. There are multiple opportunities throughout the day to write. Still, it's much less effort to jump onto FaceBook or scroll through pretty pictures on Instagram.

By doing trial-and-error experimentation before your writing sprint starts, you can pinpoint your distractions and the time of day when you'll write successfully. Then block out that time in your calendar.

Don't obsess about what to write or meeting a daily word count target during this training stage. Just focus on creating a consistent writing habit. This new habit will serve you well when it comes time to write your nonfiction book in a month.

Know What to Write

During this training period, you also want to locate the starting line and determine how to know when you've crossed the finish line. For these two things, you need a content map, which will keep you on track.

Writing nonfiction takes planning. You need to know your book's topic and your content goals. Plus, you need to know your target audience. The more planning you do before your 30-day sprint, the better prepared you'll be, and the easier it will become to meet your daily target word-count.

There's nothing more demoralizing to a writer than facing a blank page and having no idea what to write. And doing that often during a 30-day writing sprint is a sure way to fail.

Your Book-in-a-Month Success Plan

However, if you plan the content for your book's chapters before you start your sprint, you can use these as your roadmap. Consider these plans a guide, not immovable or set-in-stone.

As you write, other ideas and topics will spring to mind, and you have the flexibility to incorporate these into your project and even cut topics that become irrelevant. But you need to start out with a plan, or else you'll waste precious time wandering in the creative wilderness. That makes it difficult, if not impossible, to write a nonfiction book in 30 days.

Create a Book Outline

Before I begin a new nonfiction project, I always identify the needs of my target audience. What do they need to know? What fears are they trying to overcome? What goals do they have? What problem are they trying to solve?

Then I create a book outline that leads them to where they want to go or the result they want to get. At a minimum, the first draft of my book outline is a series of chapter headings. More often than not, it also includes a jumble of sub-headings for topics I know I need to cover.

Writing a block of content is much less overwhelming than writing a book. Once I have my chapter headings and sub-headings identified, I use these as my prompts during writing sessions. I don't have to write them in order, so if the next topic on my list doesn't inspire me, I pick one further down that does.

I like this approach because I'm cherry-picking the topics that inspire me the most, which helps keep my momentum going. When it's time to circle back to the topics I've skipped, I'm so far into the sprint I'm less likely to abandon my writing challenge. I've invested so much time and effort into it that I become determined to finish.

Use your writing time during the 30-day sprint to commit words to a page. Roll the organization and content structuring tasks into the editing phase that follows. But a good plan will make this final step easy.

Overcoming Procrastination or Writer's Block

Just because you've set a writing schedule and know what you need to write doesn't mean your success is guaranteed. Even with the best plan in the world, you'll need willpower and motivation to nudge you into the writing zone and help you cross the finish line.

There are a few different techniques you can use to increase your motivation to write. I've successfully used meditation to increase my word count and freewriting to clear my writer's block.

It took me a couple of misstarts to complete my first nonfiction book during a 30-day sprint. If you've tried and failed, don't let that discourage you from trying again. This time, success is within your grasp if you put in the training before the race.

How to Evaluate Your Book Idea's Success Potential

By Nina Amir

When writers come up with ideas for books and want simply to sit down and begin writing, it means they have enough excitement about their ideas to actually start and even finish their projects. However, that excitement may cause them to begin too quickly.

In fact, not every book idea deserves to become a book. Some ideas make better articles or essays because you don't have enough subject matter to produce a full-length book. Others might be appropriate for a book but only for purchase by your friends and family. In other words, your idea might not have a market beyond your immediate circle of influence. Or maybe your idea simply isn't unique—though it may feel fresh to you, the market is flooded with other books just like it, and it, therefore, doesn't stand a chance of commercial success.

It's a worthwhile venture to evaluate your book idea's success potential prior to writing a word—or very many words. Do this by using the publishing industry standard—the book proposal—as your guide. Take your idea and look at it through the lens of a book proposal, and you'll know soon enough if your idea has the ability to make it as a print or e-book. Evaluate your idea as any agent or acquisitions editor might if they were to read the business plan for your book. You don't need to write a proposal, just go through what I call the proposal process, or the author training process.

The Proposal Process

Book proposals contain a variety of sections. The most important ones will quickly tell you if your idea is viable:

- **Markets.** This book proposal section asks you to describe your book's markets—large groups/numbers of people who might be interested in and purchase your book. These are the people who will find your book relevant for some reason. If your idea has appeal to large markets, many markets, or even one small niche market, it might be a good idea.

- **Competing Titles.** In this proposal section you look at the previously published books and compare your book idea to them. If you feel your idea is unique and fills a "hole" on the shelf of a brick-and-mortar bookstore as well as an online bookstore, then your idea gets the green light.

- **About the Author.** In this section you actually write a bio of yourself and discuss why you are the best person to write this book. However, this is a chance to compare yourself to the authors of the competing books and ask yourself if you can compete with them. Are you unique? Do you have the credentials necessary? If so, then your idea passes on to the next part of the proposal process.

- **Mission Statement.** Do you have a reason to write this book? Is it your purpose or mission? Will your book serve a purpose, too? Will it add benefit and offer value? If you can answer "yes" to these questions, your idea might be a winner.

- **List of Chapters.** Create a table of contents for your potential book. Does it look like it has the makings for a book? Can you see an actual structure and imagine content for a full book? If "yes," proceed!

- **Chapter Summaries.** Describe each chapter's content. If you can summarize each chapter and then feel certain you really do have a book inside you that needs to get out, and it all makes sense on paper, get writing!

A book proposal includes additional sections, and all of them prove helpful to the proposal process; they train you to become a successful author. It's best to run your idea through all of them, but the sections above are the most essential for evaluating your book idea. If you take the time to go through this evaluation process, you'll write many more successful books—books that sell to readers and to publishers— and end up with a lot less "practice" manuscripts that you shove in a drawer or save on your hard drive for eternity because they just aren't marketable.

To learn how to use all the sections of a book proposal to evaluate your book through the lens of an agent or acquisitions editor, read _The Author Training Manual._

Four Questions to Help You Start Your Nonfiction Book

By Vicki C. Weiland

As with all of us who love writing and everything connected with it I also know the difficulty we all face, even daily, in actually tackling that page, rewriting that chapter, or agonizing over that one word. Yet, despite this, we all know that we have no choice—we are driven by an inner reservoir that impels us to keep on going; we must get the problem resolved! We must get those words on paper! Then there are those keenly precious moments when the words flow, when all that is deep within us comes to the surface, and the result is a page or pages of sheer delight and achievement. All of the people in our lives know the signs. They are patient when they are speaking with us and it is obvious that half our brain is focused on something other than what they are saying; they are infinitely kind when we say, "I'll only be a little while longer . . ." All of this goes with the ebb and flow of writing (and editing). It is the river of our lives.

Acknowledging all of the above, and the difficulties both internal and external that face all writers, brings me to my pet peeve, albeit a bittersweet one. My all-time pet peeve has to be the would-be writers who talk about writing every chance they get, sometimes for years and years on end . . . but who never, ever actually take that confessed desire and do anything about it. I am referring to people who never cease to remind their listeners about "that book" they want to write, and who actually have concrete ideas and a great "pitch" for it! I get hooked every time. I catch the vision. I sit up straighter. I move closer to the edge of my chair, ready to encourage and help. I come on board. "Tell me more," I say. And then, it stops. I can see it in their eyes, or rather in how they avoid my eyes. It's over for them.

I always feel sad and deflated, as much for me as for them. As a developmental editor who works in tandem with a writer, I love ideas, and I love the natural enthusiasm and vitality that comes from sharing ideas. I love following a writer's mind to see where these ideas might go. It is stimulating and enjoyable. It is creative. And, at that moment, as the dream is being shared, everything is so alive with promise.

And then, after that initial burst of euphoria and the accompanying gleam I see in their eyes once "the book" begins to take form (again), only to fizzle out (again), I can't stop wondering, "What if . . ."

What if they really sat down and started to write? What if they put their foot into the river?

4 Questions to Get You Writing and Focused

So, because I believe there is a writing voice deep within just yearning to grab onto something that will pull it out of the abyss of wishful thinking, I always offer to send them Vicki's Four Questions©. I hope they will work like a set of pliers to pry open a valve just wide enough that some words will flow out onto paper. Because I know, once they do, there will be no turning back!

Do you want to start writing, but you are not sure where to begin? In all of the years I have been a nonfiction developmental editor I have discovered that all would-be writers actually do have a precise idea of what they want to say, why they want to say it, and how they would like their book to look and feel. When it comes to starting the writing process, sometimes they just need a little help getting their feet wet. I'd like to offer you that help by asking you to try your hand at answering Vicki's Four Questions©:

1. What is your vision of the book? (What are the three most important qualities, i.e., elegant, academic, thought-provoking, informative, authoritative, reflective, "change the world," dramatic, etc.?)

2. What is the most important thing you want readers to have learned after they have read your book?

3. What would you most like readers to feel when they close your book?

4. What three words would you like most for a book reviewer to say about your book?

The Purpose of the Questions

Happily, in addition to getting your creative energy flowing, each of these questions also has an overall editorial purpose that I hope will prove helpful:

- Question number one addresses your desired "author's voice" and the overall "tone" you would like the book to convey.

- Question number two provides the "focus" for the book, and it is also the backbone for developing an outline so as to incrementally educate and drive the reader through the content.

- Question number three is the "heart-line" that will flow throughout the book. It is your deeply desired outcome for writing the book.

- Question number four motivates you to think about marketing—who your readers are and what would motivate them to buy your book.

While I developed these questions for books, they can also be applied to an article or an essay. This month, as you progress in the writing of your nonfiction piece, you might consider keeping your answers nearby so that you can look back on them regularly to see if you are still "on track." If not, you may want to begin to hone in on them again. Or you may find that your original concept has changed and is crystallizing into something new. If that is the case, then you may want to ask yourself the questions again.

Most of all, I hope they will stimulate you to move ahead with your dream and to turn that dream into reality! It is exciting to embark upon this adventure of writing, and to take what is in your head and heart and create a lasting piece of work.

Seven Questions to Ask
If You Want to Write Nonfiction

By Roger C. Parker

I've been excited about the annual National Nonfiction Writing Month 30-day challenge ever since I first discovered it several years ago. It's a dynamite idea that's only improved each year.

What founder Nina Amir obviously recognized, and the accomplishments of her participants proves, is that authors need challenges and deadlines in order to succeed!

Writing is really hard when you don't have a starting point and you don't have a finish line!

—Without a starter's pistol, it's too easy to procrastinate getting started, so years can go by without writing a book that could make a big difference in your life.

—Without a finish line, it's too hard to establish and maintain the habit of consistent daily progress necessary to finishing your book on time (so you can turn your efforts to editing the devil out of your first draft).

Questions to Ask Yourself before Starting to Write

Your success writing a book in a month depends a lot on how well prepared you are; experience has shown that asking the right questions is the easiest way to prepare to write.

Asking, and answering, questions like the following increases the alignment between your book and your long-term life and career goals. The questions also encourage you to re-examine your goals and work as efficiently as possible.

1. Why do you want to write a book?

2. Who are your "ideal readers?"

3. How will readers benefit from your book?

4. Why should readers choose your book over the competition?

5. How can write more efficiently?

6. How will readers discover your book?

7. How will you profit from your book?

As you can see from the above, the questions themselves are deceptively simple. But answering them is like peeling back the layers of an onion; each layer reveals another layer of options and opportunities.

How Questions Lead to Options and Opportunities

The first question, "Why do you want to write a book?" for example, is a reality check that encourages you to examine the role that your book will play in your life. Are you writing for pleasure, to drive business, or for personal brand and career advancement?

Question 5, "How can you write more efficiently?" invites you to consider ways to simplify your writing tasks. Options include choosing a title that provides a structure for writing each chapter, like _Key Management Models: The 60+ Models Every Manager Needs to Know._ Selecting a functional title like this simplifies your writing and reduces stress by placing the emphasis on choosing the right 60 models, and it defines the amount you need to write about each model.

The question also encourages you to explore ways to share the writing responsibilities by engaging others as contributors, co-authors, or ghostwriters. Looking for ways to be more efficient also encourages you to explore ways to set up your computer's hard drive for easy file access and back-up. It also prompts you to save time in the future by avoiding manuscript-formatting errors as you write.

Books and Business Plans

Finally, Question 7, "How will you profit from your book?" forces you to address the business side of publishing by looking beyond income from book sales (the traditional metric of writing success). It puts the emphasis on viewing your book as a new business, which requires a business plan to succeed.

Often, authors focus on writing the right book, rather than viewing their books as future profit-generating tools. In today's market, most books are investments in the future. You're trading time, now, for profits later. Taking the time to specify how your marketing funnel will attract readers and convert them into clients will help you avoid disappointment down the road.

Tips for Answering the Seven Questions

Here are some suggestions to help you get the maximum benefit from your answers:

- **Write out your answers.** Don't feel you have to always be typing on a keyboard. Look for resources that allow you to engage more of your senses by writing by hand, often away from your computer.

- **Dig deeper.** Don't be satisfied by your first response. Return to the questions and approach them from a fresh perspective. Look for the "questions behind the questions."

- **Keep everything together.** This includes your answers to the 7 questions and the questions that you want to ask experts like Nina, who are committed to a 30-day writing challenge. Look for tools, like worksheets and workbooks you can print on 3-hole paper and save in a 3-ring binder.

Why Now Is the Time to Begin, or Rejuvenate, Your Writing Career

This is the best time ever to write a nonfiction book. You have more resources available to help you than ever before.

Consider: when I wrote my first bestselling nonfiction book, _Looking Good in Print: A Guide to Basic Design for Desktop Publishing (The Ventana Press Looking Good Series)_, which sold over 350,000 copies around the world, or my "for Dummies" books, (which sold even more), there was an absence of writing and publishing resources to guide me through the ins and outs of the writing nonfiction for profit field.

With this eBook, you benefit from Nina's experience and the experience of her extended network of writing and published experts, who contributed to this guide. Plus, you have her other writing guides and a plethora of writing resources that have been published to date.

Twelve Ways to Organize Your Book Ideas

By Roger C. Parker

To write a nonfiction book as efficiently as possible, you need to start by organizing your ideas.

Starting to write a book without a content plan is an invitation to false starts and wasted effort. It's as foolish as trying to drive from New Hampshire to San Diego without referring to a road map, intending to navigate entirely by intuition. You may end up there, but you may have wasted a lot of time (and gasoline) on unnecessary detours and dead ends.

You don't have to know exactly what you're going to write about in each paragraph of every chapter. But, for maximum productivity, you do need to know:

- The title of each chapter.
- The premise, or big idea, of each chapter.
- The main points, supporting facts, or steps you intend to write about in each chapter.

Likewise, if you're intending to blog a book, you need an editorial calendar for your blog posts to guide you and keep your blog posts on schedule so your book will appear on time.

Why You Need a Plan

If you start to write without a content plan, you're likely to waste a lot of valuable time staring at a blank screen. This will be because you're trying to simultaneously figure out what you want to write while trying to write. The result? You'll probably spend more time worrying and less time writing.

With a plan, however, even a loose plan, you'll be more likely to be able to immediately start writing as you start to write each chapter.

Partly, this will be because planning engages your brain. As a result, while you were driving, sleeping, or relaxing, your brain will be thinking about your upcoming chapters, searching for ideas, and making connections—preparing for your next writing session.

Planning Tools

There is no, single "right way" for everyone to organize their ideas into a properly sequenced series of chapters. What might be an invigorating, efficient process—or habit—for one person can be frustrating and nonproductive for another.

There are two types of planning tools you can use to organize your ideas: low-tech tools and computer-based tools. In the right hands, either approach can be very valuable for organizing your ideas into a writing plan for blogging your book.

In fact, there's nothing wrong with coming up with your own approach that combines elements of both approaches.

Low-Tech Organizing Tools

There's a time and a place for "hands on" tools, even in the computer age!

1. **Sketches.** An excellent starting point is to hand-draw a sketch showing the sequence of the topics you want to include in

your book. Authors owe a debt of gratitude to Dan Roam for legitimizing the power of sketches to simplify complex ideas in his groundbreaking book, _The Back of the Napkin: Solving Problems and Selling Ideas with Pictures_. Many of my articles and books begin as sketches on yellow legal paper, although you can also sketch on poster-sized sheets of paper or draw on white boards using dry-erase markers.

2. **Lists & outlines.** After sketching out the "big picture" of your book, the next step can be to expand your sketch listing the main idea and key supporting points for each chapter. There's something satisfying about writing with a narrow felt-tip marker on a fresh page, fleshing out each topic with information and ideas I want to share.

3. **Index cards.** Index cards are another time-proven writing tool. Index cards come in a variety of sizes, 3 by 5, 4 by 6, and 5 by 8 inches. Index cards are a favorite of authors like John McPhee, who is known for plastering the walls of his office with cards displaying the structure of his current projects. Each card contains a single idea that is then inserted into the right location. In a New Yorker article describing his writing process, John McPhee described how he doesn't begin to write until he's placed each card in its correct location. In your case, you simplify this technique by devoting a single index card to each blog post, so you can easily sort and resort the cards until the posts are in a logical order.

4. **Sticky notes.** Sticky notes build on the idea of sketches by providing an easy way to identify and organize supporting ideas. Add just one idea or supporting detail to each sticky note, then attach the sticky notes to your "big picture" sketch or the index cards for each of your blog posts. An added benefit; you can use different-colored sticky notes to color code different categories of ideas.

5. **Hanging folders.** A surprising number of the high-productivity authors and writers I've interviewed continue to use low-tech tools like hanging folders to organize and store ideas and sketches appearing in a variety of media, such as index cards, legal pads, photocopies, screen captures, and printed manuscript pages. (I, myself, like 3-ring binders with tabbed dividers.) Whether your folders are used for chapters in a book, different content marketing projects, or "unassigned" resources and ideas, it's nice to have a simple, "high-touch" way of accessing and organizing ideas.

Software and Internet-Based Organizing Tools

The primary advantage of the following software-based tools is that, after organizing your ideas, you can export your work to your word processing program. This saves you time, because you don't have to enter, or re-type, the ideas from your sketches, index cards, or lists into your word processing programs.

8. **List and outlining tools.** Using a word processing program, like Microsoft Word, you can use their lists and outlining features to create a detailed action plan for your blogged book or book. For example, after creating a 2-column or 3-column table, you can use Word's Table>Sort feature to sort the titles as well as the topics intended for each chapter. The advantage of using your word processing software for organizing your blog posts is that there's no learning curve involved, and you can easily copy and paste the ideas associated with each topic into your blogging software program.

9. **Spreadsheets.** Another option is to use a spreadsheet program, like Microsoft Excel, to plan your book. The process is similar: in the first column, enter the title for each blog post or chapter. In the second column, summarize the main idea associated with the title. In the third column, enter the ideas and examples you want to include. You can then sort your spreadsheet and copy and paste each topic's ideas into your word processing software.

10. **Drawing programs.** If the idea of sketching, described earlier, appeals to you, you'll like that there are many low-cost drawing programs available that will allow you to sketch out your contents of your book and enter the ideas associated with each chapter. This idea is especially useful if you have a mobile device, like an iPhone, iPad, or Android device. Drawing programs for mobile applications are extremely inexpensive, often available for less than $5.

11. **Mind maps.** Mind mapping software, like Mindjet's MindManager, take the idea of sketching to the next level. Mind mapping has been used as creativity tool for over 25 years, and mind mapping software has been available for over 10 years. Mind mapping allows you unprecedented power to create detailed maps of all of your writing projects, collapsing and expanding your maps to display as much, or as little, of the details associated with your projects as desired. Mindjet also allows you to enter start dates and deadlines for each of your chapters, helping you keep your writing on schedule.

12. **Storyboards.** Another software-based option is to create storyboards for your chapters using popular presentation programs like Microsoft PowerPoint. Create a separate slide or presentation visual for each of your chapters, adding the main ideas you want to include in each chapter as items in a bulleted list. By devoting one slide to each chapter, you can use PowerPoint's SlideSorter feature to rearrange the order of the chapters before exporting the presentation to your word processor.

13. **Transcription.** Smartphones and handy dictation units make it easy to capture ideas, even if you're too busy to write them down. Several of the authors I've interviewed come up with their best ideas while driving or stopped at traffic lights. When an idea appears, they can immediately email their idea to themselves, call their office and leave a message, or record their idea using today's low-cost voice recognition systems.

14. **Cloud computing.** Other options for organizing your book include organizing your ideas using remote file hosting services like <u>Dropbox</u> or <u>Evernote</u>. The advantage of these solutions is that you can immediately access your work from any online computer, from home, office, or while traveling. Evernote is an especially popular alternative because you can tag and search for items by keywords or attributes. You can also call in your ideas, and they will be translated and added to the files containing your blog post ideas.

Getting Ready to Write Your Book

Before you start to write your book, take the time to try out the various approaches to organizing your ideas.

Explore more than one option and see what works best for you. The sooner you come up with your own efficient way of organizing your ideas before you begin writing, the sooner you can embark on your journey to writing your book!

Mind Map Your Project from Start to Finish

By Nina Amir

Before you start any book project, you must know what you plan to write about. You need to develop a table of contents, or a list of your planned chapters. You must decide what will be in those chapters—the actual content. At no time is this more important than when you write a nonfiction book in a month.

One of the best ways to make these decisions involves using a process called mind mapping. You can do this by hand using a large piece of white paper and colored pens, or a computer program, such as Freemind. (This program is free; you can purchase better ones, like MindNode which I use.) Some people also like to use Post-It notes or white boards. If you choose to use Post-It notes, write the words and phrases on the notes, and stick them on a poster board or even on something larger.

No matter the technique you decide to use, I typically call it a "brain dump." I've often heard it described as "vomiting" your ideas onto a page and then cleaning them up.

How to Do a Mind Map

Here's how mind mapping works:

1. Get a large, blank piece of paper—the bigger the better.

2. In the center of the paper, print your project's topic or subject. Draw a circle around the keyword or phrase. (For example, if you are writing a book on the topic of how to train dogs, you might use the key-phrase "dog training."

3. Now write down the first word or phrase that pops into your mind (for example, "stay"). This may become a subtopic that constitutes a chapter in your book. Or it could be a subheading in one of your chapters or in your article. Don't worry about that now, though.

4. Jot down the next word that comes to mind (for example, "tips," "down," "on leash," "off leash," "punishment, "reward," or "come"). These all represent possible sub topics (chapters) or sub-subtopics (subheadings) in your book.

5. Repeat step four until you've run out of word associations.

6. Now go back and draw lines from your topic (keyword or phrase) to the words or phrases you think should be chapters (or subheadings) in your book. Circle these phrases. Then somehow indicate which other words or phrases belong with this chapter or subheading. (This is where your colored pens come in. You can color code different items, draw colored lines, make colored circles or boxes, etc.) The sticky note method works well at this stage because you can move them around for organizational purposes.

For the more organized person, another way to do this involves grouping subtopics and sub-subtopics together as you do the mind mapping exercise. Here's how this would work using the same example above.

1. In the center of the paper, print your project's topic or subject. Draw a circle around the keyword or phrase (for example, "dog training").

2. Draw a line from your keyword and write down the first word or phrase that pops into your mind (for example, "stay").

Circle the word or phrase. This is a subtopic that may become a chapter in your book or a subheading.

3. Now draw a line from that word and jot down the next word that comes to mind (for example, "tips"). This represents a sub-subtopic, or a subheading in your chapter.

4. Repeat step three until you've run out of word associations.

5. Now, return to your keyword or key phrase and repeat the exercise. Come up with another subtopic, then as many word associations (sub-subtopics) with that subtopic as possible, and then move on to another.

6. Continue until you have created 10 to 15 subtopics, each with several sub-subtopics.

This produces a fairly well organized mind map. You can still color code it if you like.

Create Your Book Structure

Now, take the related subtopics and sub-subtopics and arrange them into a table of contents. It will look like this:

Book Topic (your book's title and subtitle)

Chapter 1 Subtopic (chapter title)

    Sub-subtopic (subheading)

    Sub-subtopic

    Sub-subtopic

Chapter 2 Subtopic (chapter title)

    Sub-subtopic (subheading)

    Sub-subtopic

    Sub-subtopic

When you finish your mind map, you'll have the structure or outline for your book, and you'll know if you have enough content for a book. With this guide, you also are ready to begin writing.

Using a Mind Map to Plan Your Nonfiction Book

By Roger C. Parker

The easiest and fastest way you can plan your nonfiction book is to use a mind map. Mind mapping is a technique you can use on paper, on whiteboards, or you can use a variety of computer software for Macs, PCs, iPhones, and iPads.

What is a mind map?

Mind maps resemble the solar system, with the sun in the center and the planets revolving around it.

Since we're talking about nonfiction books, the center graphic will contain the title of your nonfiction book. Surrounding it are subtopics—each containing the title of one of the sections, or parts, of your book.

Each of the section graphics links to smaller subtopics—each one representing one of the chapters in your book.

Finally, the last step, is to add the main ideas—or sub-subtopics—you intend to cover in each chapter. You can explore and download free PDF examples of mind maps of current nonfiction books here, here, and here.

Mind Mapping Benefits

When you've finished a mind map, you'll have a graphic that displays the "big picture" of your book—the sections and chapters—as well as the main ideas and contents of each chapter.

If you're using software like MindManager on your computer, you can control your view of the project by collapsing and expanding the map:

- Collapsing a mind map means displaying only the "big picture" sections and chapters of your book. This permits you to analyze the sequence and flow of your ideas. When you collapse a topic, a small icon appears, reminding you that that the topic contains additional information.

- Expanding a mind map occurs when you press the "collapsed" icon. This reveals the previously-hidden subtopics.

One of the big advantages of working with mind mapping software is that you can share your work with others. Once you have created a mind map of your book's table of contents, you can share copies with agents, co-authors, co-workers, editors, and publishers. Mind map files can be shared as email attachments or placed online for others to add their comments.

Export is another major benefit offered by mind mapping software. Once you've completed the mind map of your book, you can export it to your word processing program, eliminating the need to retype what you've already written.

Planning Your Nonfiction Book

Here's how I suggest you use a mind mapping software program to plan and write your nonfiction book this November:

1. **Organize your ideas.** Start by adding your book's proposed title in the center of the map, and—just as a starting point—add three subtopics for the main sections of your book (beginning,

middle, and end). Then, add four chapter subtopics to each section. As you plan your book, insert the titles of each of the 12 chapters. Then, add subtopics to each chapter identifying the main ideas of each chapter. Put your map aside overnight. The next day, drag ideas from one chapter to another, or add new ideas or delete unwanted ideas. Change the order of the chapters if necessary. When you're finished, you'll have a detailed table of contents for your book.

2. **Schedule your work.** The next step is crucial. It's not enough to plan your book. You have to write your book, and this requires creating your own deadlines for each chapter. Without specific writing deadlines, all you have are intentions, not commitments. Most mind mapping software programs allow you to add start dates and deadlines to each topic. These provide a visual commitment and timetable for writing your book.

3. **Track your progress.** Finally, use your mind map as a motivational tool by showing your progress as you move forward. Each time you complete a topic, you can add a finished icon—or small visual symbol—to the topic, or you can indicate completion by changing the color of the topic or deleting the topic. You'll feel a definite sense of progress as you add completion dates or finished icons to each topic!

Getting Started with Mind Mapping

There are over 100 mind mapping software programs available for computers and mobile devices. Pricing is all over the map, from free to several hundred dollars. Some programs are entirely web-based and charge small monthly payments.

The best idea is to search online for mind mapping software. Follow blogs like Chuck Frey's <u>Mind Mapping Software Blog</u>, the <u>Mindjet blog</u>, and my <u>Published & Profitable Writer's Tips</u> Blog that contains frequent mind mapping examples and tips, plus upcoming events for authors.

A Powerful Tool

Mind mapping can make a major contribution to the success of any nonfiction author. It boosts creativity and keeps you focused and on schedule while saving you time. Best of all, you can't really go wrong, because most mind mapping software can import and export files to different formats. As a result, you're not locked into a specific program when you get started mind mapping on your computer or mobile device.

Mining Your Memories
to Write Memoir

By Linda Joy Myers

Writers often struggle with the issue of memory: Do I have enough memories to write a memoir? Are my memories "correct?" What if someone disagrees—will I be found out or exposed like James Frey was?

The answer is no! There is no such thing as correct memory; it's all about perception and interpretation. Everyone's view of an event is like a slice of pie—each section looks toward the middle from a different angle. Everyone in a family would write a different memoir—if they dared! (And the James Frey thing was not about memory; it was about exaggerating.)

There are many ways to capture your memories. Memories exist as wisps of perfume, snippets of images, stories that haunt our dreams, fragments of our lives waiting for us to breathe full life into them so they can unfold on the screen of story.

Streams of memory arise when we hear a song or when smells and sounds remind us of certain moments. You can look for these streams by doing research: Visit your hometown where there is history and meaning, memories around every corner. When I first started exploring my past, I took the long trek to visit the town where I grew up in Oklahoma. As the familiar lay of the land, the rise of the wheat elevators, the smells of earth rose up, I was shocked and amazed at the rush of images, like a movie in fast motion, as I drove down familiar roads. My body knew this as home and triggered more memories than I could have imagined, fueling my need to capture them before they just as easily flew away.

To encourage your memories, look at photographs, listen to a song, explore where your town is on Google Earth. Research is a great way to get started. Then place your fingers over the keyboard and invite images and snippets to flow from your fingers. You can begin with a piece of story, an image, a sensual experience—listen to your body/mind as the story takes shape, and take dictation!

Begin with a scene. Put yourself in a time and a place, setting where you are physically. This helps you to write directly from sensual experience. Write from who you were at different ages.

Use dreams to help you get into your stories and memories. Write down your dreams, and then keep writing, free associating, exploring. Sometimes insights and connections happen when we aren't trying.

Dive into the tough memories—the stories that scare you, the stories you really don't want to write. It is here that the gold is found, the moments in your life that you need to understand, your secrets and regrets. What are the life lessons that haunt you, that come back to you on soft feet in the middle of the night? These contain some of the important points of your life, the times that tug at your heart and soul. There are riches there for you to explore.

Memoir writing is about capturing who we are and were. We need to be honest, to write our truths as best we can, not worrying about a publisher, the public, an agent, or even the family. We have to be true to ourselves. The best stories are the deepest truths that we can share as we dig into what it means to be human, what it's like to travel our own unique path. In the current marketplace, if and when you're interested in publishing, people are eager to learn from others—a memoir invites people into their own living room, even their hearts—and in this we all become deeply intertwined in the shared stories of human experience.

Tips for Capturing Significant Memories

1. Write down memories on envelopes at the market, in the car—parked of course, or taking a walk. Call yourself and leave a message. Text it to someone. Take a note on your cell phone. If you don't write it down, it disappears.

2. Get out photo albums. Use the photo as a trigger to write. Write about what you were feeling. Write about what happened before and after the photo was taken.

3. Describe the photo in detail, and muse about its meaning, what's hidden that the viewer can't see. If it's a photo of long dead relatives, but it fascinates you, write what you imagine happened on that day. Weave in family stories.

4. Talk with friends, and write down what you remember together.

5. Family events can be triggers for your memoir file. Write things down or put them on tape.

6. If you have a computer, surf the web for memoir writing sites, memory preservation sites, war stories. It's all out there.

7. Write for 10 minutes, a short vignette.

8. Next time, write for 20 minutes. Notice that the more you write, the more you write!

9. Basic rule: do not throw away anything. Do not hit the delete key. Make a folder called "saved early drafts." Don't listen to that inner critic. It doesn't yet know what you are about. Fear and shame are friends of the inner critic. If these are parts of you, then beware of any little voice that tells you to throw your writing away. It's most often wrong. Besides, computer files don't take up much room. Keep your stories—they are part of your research and your journey.

10. Invite dreams, favorite memories, and unforgettable moments. Allow them to flow through you in a free write—writing for

15 minutes without taking your fingers off the keys or your hand from the page. Get into the flow—it helps develop your writing stamina.

11. Don't worry about where to start or what you will write about. Write short vignettes to quilt together later.

12. Remember, you have your own story. Don't let the point of view of family members interfere with writing YOUR story.

13. Childhood can be a treasure of all kinds of memories, both good and bad. Allow yourself to be in the body and in the sensory experience of the child, and take dictation. Notice voice, details, and language, and write in the flow of what you remember.

Plot, Structure, and Theme
in Your Memoir

By Linda Joy Myers

When we begin writing a memoir, we find ourselves traveling down bumpy roads and misty memory paths as we search for our story. We feel the urgency to capture a place, a time, people, and special moments, somehow gathering a time that is forever gone and creating it again on the page. Every memoir writer is writing for a reason, and often a passionate one. It might be to bring someone they loved to life again, as I did with my great-grandmother, Blanche, when I put her back in the garden to swear at the weeds or feed me a ripe strawberry right off the vine. Or the memoirist is writing to find words to explore shock and grief, as Joan Didion does in her memoir *The Year of Magical Thinking,* or as Isabel Allende does in a different way in *Paula: A Memoir,* the book she wrote as she tended her dying daughter. Michael Chabon explores fatherhood in his memoir, and Ruth Reichel entertains us about her family and food in a series of memoirs.

A memoir might be a gift to a child or grandchild, a legacy that is supposed to tell some of the tales of the past, as Dorothy Allison does in *Two or Three Things I Know for Sure,* and many war memoirs do. Vera Brittain in *Testament of Youth* chronicles the sleepy villages in England before all the young men eagerly enlisted in WWI, young men like her brother, her fiancé, and many of her friends. Her memoir shows as nothing else could the intimate experience of growing up with boys who turn into men, all of whom are killed before their 20th birthday.

Most memoirists that I meet have stories roiling around in their heads, but they find it difficult to set them, to locate the story in the world of black ink on a white page. Over the last few years of memoir writing and teaching, I have found that certain techniques are helpful in grounding the story enough to get hold of it. The stories that roam about in our minds are fluid and tricky things, hard to pin down, and they keep changing like images in a kaleidoscope.

Turning Points and Timeline Exercise

There is a great technique that helps you locate the main spine of your stories for a longer memoir. Think about the turning point moments in your life, the special times that changed you profoundly and altered your life in such a way that it was never the same again. Make a list of the 10-15 most significant moments that turned your life path from one direction to another. These might be very different kinds of moments, some ecstatic joy and soaring happiness, and others profound sadness, confusion, or grief.

Now draw a timeline on an 18x24 sheet of paper—a long horizontal line to represent time, and mark your birth about one quarter of the way along that line. This way you can note the events that you might want to write that occur before your birth. You might want to write the stories of family, parents, or grandparents—some of the lore that you listened to during holidays or family picnics.

Divide the horizontal line into sections that represent decades, and set out the dates of your life, beginning with your birth, including the year and the date along the horizontal line. Begin to locate your turning point events along the timeline.

In my workshops, there is always an "aha" when doing this exercise. First, thinking about the significant turning points can be illuminating and provide new insights, but then when people see events on the timeline, inevitably they start murmuring about how the events clustered, or how they'd thought the event was closer or further away from another significant event. The emotional impact of the timeline exercise can be powerful, as there is nothing like an image to illuminate the important moments of our lives to offer new insights.

Theme

A memoir is a focused story about a theme—a topic, an angle the story will take to show important changes in the protagonist—you—and the reason that the story is being told. When we start writing, we often don't know our theme—we are still marinating in the memories and details of our stories. When we explore the turning point moments and muse again about why we are writing a memoir, theme begins to rise up like mountains at the edge of the plains. This is often an unconscious process, and we need to write some stories before theme becomes clearer.

An example of theme: _Lit_, by Mary Karr, is the third volume of her trilogy of memoirs. This last book is about her descent into and her recovery from alcoholism through finding religion. It's about many other things too—her early literary life, her husband, son, and friends who helped her. It's about her mother and her family and her deeper reflections on material she wrote in _The Liars' Club_. But the arc of the story takes us from her being lost in using alcohol to numb herself, to becoming sober and finding herself again.

Most of you know that Frank McCourt's _Angela's Ashes: A Memoir_ is about his poverty-stricken childhood in Limerick, Ireland. The arc of his story begins with his earliest memories and ends with his leaving his home to come to New York. There are other themes and topics too— the Catholic Church, death, his mother Angela, his abandoning father, and dying, starving siblings. If you look at the book in terms of turning points, you will see that he includes what he considers significant events that shift the plot into new directions, each one adding force and direction to the trajectory of the story.

Plot

What is a plot? A plot is a series of dramatized events that show how characters encounter obstacles and challenges, and how they solve their problems. The protagonist is different by the end of the book than he is at the beginning.

The arc of the narrative can be divided into Act One, Two, and Three, the usually invisible structure of a book, play, or movie, though in a play this structure is overt. In Act One, the characters are introduced, the story problem is set up, and we are drawn into the world of the story.

In Act Two, all the problems of the characters become more muddled and complex, and there are a series of actions and reactions that show the development of the character's journey to change and transformation, all the while trying to solve the problems that were delineated at the beginning. Since real life does become more complicated, the way that plot works is imitated by life. Or is it the other way around?

In Act Three, the threads and layers of development reach a peak at the crisis and climax of the story. Here the character is tested, where the true depth of learning and transformation is revealed. The crisis may be thought of as a spiritual challenge or a "dark night of the soul" where the deepest beliefs and core truths of the character are tested. The climax is the highest level of tension and conflict that the protagonist must resolve as the story comes to a close. There's an "aha" at the end, an epiphany when the main character has learned her lessons and can never return to the previous way of living.

Dramatic structure, the narrative arc, is a mythic structure, a deeply satisfying resolution that fits with our need to create pattern and perspective in the midst of the chaos of real life. That is why memoir is so challenging—we are trying to create story out of chaos, to make sense of the irrational and nonsensical impulses that drive all human beings. When you lift your own significant plot moments out of the confusion, you will have the basic spine of your story.

A memoir brings the light of our own consciousness and our reflections to the simplicity of the "this happened and that happened" episodic structure that is often the first draft version of the memoir. When you create your plot and become aware of your themes, you offer readers your unique perspective, shining your creative, artistic light on "reality" so they can be inspired and transformed by your story.

Develop the Energy to
Write a Book in a Month

By Nina Amir

Energy. Few writing teachers or book coaches speak about how your physiology affects your ability to write. In fact, energy affects every aspect of your success as a writer. But never is this truer than when you have a deadline looming over your head—a deadline like finishing a book in a month.

Many writers who decide to start and finish a book in 30 days begin strong and steadily lose steam as the month goes on. Their energy wanes and with it their motivation and creativity.

But that doesn't have to happen to you if you pay attention to your energy and do everything possible to keep it high and positive.

Three Types of Energy that Affect Your Writing

Three types of energy affect your ability to write productively. They are:

1. Emotional Energy

2. Mental Energy

3. Physical Energy

Let's look at each one individually. Keep in mind, however, that each type of energy has an impact on the other. For example, if your emotional energy is low or negative, your physical energy and mental energy follow suit. If your physical energy is high, your emotional and mental energy will rise as well, and you will feel more positive, clear, and focused.

Emotional Energy

Your emotions impact your energy in many ways. If you feel sad, depressed, angry, or worried, you will find your energy decreases. The stronger the negative emotions, the less physical and mental energy you have at your disposal to write.

Think about it… If you broke up with your boyfriend, got scolded at work, or are wondering how to pay your bills, how do you feel? If you sit down to write feeling that way, you won't bring high or positive energy to your writing block. Instead, you will feel tired, negative, and unfocused. And you won't write productively because your energy is so low.

When you increase your emotional energy by consciously bringing joy and enthusiasm to your work, you find yourself much more effective during writing periods. Additionally, if you can switch from negativity to positivity, you'll be more creative and productive.

You can change your emotional state quickly by changing your physical state, such as by exercising or getting out in nature. Additionally, you can change your emotional energy by changing your thoughts. Focus on something that makes you feel good and notice how your emotional (and physical) energy changes for the better.

Mental Energy

Behind every emotion lies a thought. Some say thoughts arise from emotions, but it is commonly believed that your thoughts are where your emotions—and emotional energy—are born. Therefore, if you want to increase your energy, change your thoughts first.

You know this is true. When you dwell on the "constructive" criticism your editor gave you or the rejection you received from a publisher, your emotional state changes. It becomes negative.

As your emotional state become negative, your energy drops. You get lethargic, sleepy, and lackluster.

To increase your emotional and physical energy, focus your thoughts –your mind–on the new agent you just landed, the paycheck you received for an article you wrote or the positive feedback your blog readers gave you recently. Think about your favorite place or how happy you felt during dinner with your friend or spouse. When you do so, your emotions and your energy change for the better. That means the key to changing how you feel lies in changing how you think.

Transforming habitual thought patterns can be tough. You've trained your mind to tell you how you have nothing to write about, no one will want to read your work, you don't write well, or you will be judged on the message you've shared. Now you must break those patterns.

How do you break these negative mental patterns? Begin journaling and notice when your mind takes you somewhere negative—and your emotions and energy go there, too. Pay attention to your speech; what negative things do you tell yourself daily? And how do you feel when you say those things to yourself?

Try using affirmations, positive statements that replace your negative thoughts. But don't just write them. Say them as declarations—with emotion and energy.

You also can pick an anthem for yourself. Sing songs with happy and positive messages! Or substitute the lyrics of a song you like with your affirmations. Then, sing it often!

Meditation helps, too. Let the negative thoughts go. Mentally speak to yourself in a positive manner, and visualize the future you desire.

Physical Energy

Underlying everything you do—including writing—is the need for physical energy. If you aren't rested, hydrated, and healthy, you'll find it difficult to do anything, including write.

That's why you must care for yourself—even when a deadline makes it tough to take time away from your writing work.

Here are some necessities for optional physical energy. Each one impacts your emotional and mental energy as well.

- Sleep enough—seven to eight hours per day.

- Eat three healthy meals per day.

- Eat healthy snacks.

- Drink a lot of water.

- Breathe deeply every hour.

- Take frequent breaks (one ever 50 to 60 minutes).

- Rest your eyes and mind with meditation.

- Exercise—even if it's just a 30-minute walk each day.

Give your body what it needs to function at an optimal level. If you provide your brain with the oxygen and hydration (water) it needs, you'll be more focused, clear, productive, and creative. If you care for your body by consistently being well rested and eating a healthy diet, you'll be able to work for extended periods without feeling tired or having difficulty thinking. And if you move your body often and regularly, you'll be happier and come to your desk feeling strong and able to tackle your project.

You know this is true. When you are sick or have gotten a minimal amount of sleep the night before, you struggle to write.

Exercise has been proven to change your mood. Movement can work as a meditation as well. As you move, you lose the negative thoughts and generate more positive ones, which improves your mental and emotional energy.

What Type of Energy Impacts Your Writing?

What type of energy do you think impacts your writing most often? Keep track on a daily basis and make a note of it. Then put some new energy habits in place to help you combat your energy dips. For instance, you can:

- Take work breaks every 50 minutes.

- Increase your intake of water; drink a glass every hour.

- Exercise daily.

- Sleep seven or eight hours per night minimum.

- Nap when you don't feel rested.

- Meditate—even if it's for two minutes before you begin to write.

- Journal.

- Create an affirmation practice.

- Develop energy raising triggers, like listening to a positive song before you begin to write.

There are so many ways to manage your emotional, mental and physical energy. Choose a few! Anything you do to increase your energy impacts your writing in positive ways.

Five Must-Have Habits for Writing a Book in a Month

By Nina Amir

Good habits make for productive writing. But never do you need good habits more than when you set out to write a nonfiction book in a month. In fact, whenever you set a tight deadline and want to start and finish a writing project on time, you must evaluate and improve five specific habits.

Your current habits have helped you achieve your current level of success. If you want to reach a higher level of success, change or improve your habits. Even if you are happy with your current level of success, consider what it would be like to have even greater success as a writer. What might you achieve?

What would that take? Better habits.

Level up your habits, level up your success. Better habits equate to a greater ability to meet your goals—including writing a nonfiction book in 30 days.

The following five must-have habits will help you complete the Write Nonfiction in November Challenge or any writing project you want to finish fast.

Habit #1: Consistently use your calendar.

It's amazing how many people—and writers—do not use a calendar except to record and remember doctor's appointments. Make the calendar, which means either a physical or virtual daily scheduling tool, your accountability partner.

At the beginning of every week (or month), get out your calendar and block time for writing. You could block out an hour or two Monday through Friday starting at 7 a.m. and three hours on Saturday afternoon beginning at 2 p.m., for instance. These blocks become appointments, just like going to the dentist, meeting with your personal trainer, or getting your hair cut. Imagine that changing these appointments costs you money . . . every time! (In other words, it should feel painfully difficult to miss a writing appointment with yourself.)

Every morning, review your calendar and schedule for the day. Adjust as necessary to get in your writing time. If you prefer, review your calendar the night before.

To ensure you don't "miss" some commitment because it wasn't on your calendar and, therefore, also miss your writing appointment, put everything on your calendar. Yes, everything. That means your workouts, grocery shopping trips, lunch dates with friends, time when you check email or respond to blog comments, and even dinner, phone calls, and morning rituals.

Habit #2: Write daily.

Writing must become a habit. After all, writers write—not occasionally but daily. When you start writing on a regular basis, you train yourself to produce written work consistently. You create a writing habit.

Choose a day and time for your writing blocks. As much as possible, stick to this schedule (and put in on your calendar). Try writing for the same amount of time daily, too. But even if you can't write for that amount of time sometimes, write...even a little.

For those who say they have no time to write, I recommend starting with short blocks of time—15 or 30 minutes per day. You can increase the amount of time as you get in the habit of writing. But write every day.

Habit #3: Develop a daily word-count goal.

If you want to write a book in a month, you need an idea of the number of words you must produce per day. Otherwise, you could end up short at the end of the month, which means your manuscript won't be complete.

To develop a daily word count, determine the length of your book-in-a-month project. Then do a few writing tests; see how many words you produce in 30 or 60 minutes.

Now, divide the estimated words count of your finished project by the number of hours you plan to write each day during the month. You then will know how many words you need to produce in an hour. For instance, if you want to complete a 50,000-word book in 30 hours (one hour per day for 30 days), you must be able to produce 1,666 words in 60 minutes. If you can't do that, increase the amount of time you set aside on your calendar daily to write. Use your word-count tests to decide on the length of your writing blocks.

Keep track daily of whether you meet your world-count goals. If you don't, adjust the amount of time you write each day or week.

Habit #4: Set priorities.

If you don't get around to writing or life seems to always get in the way (come first) of writing, you haven't prioritized writing. It's time to make this activity your #1 priority—at while writing a book in a month.

If writing never becomes your priority, everything else always comes first. And your book won't get written even if you plan to write it during a longer period of time. That's why writing and your writing project must feel so important that they take precedence or becomes a must-do item every day.

I get it . . . You have kids or elderly parents to care for, and, of course, they often need to come first. You have a job with deadlines and demands. But if you use your calendar and schedule your writing blocks, you can, in most cases, make writing a priority—and treat it as such. You can write consistently.

Writing first thing in the morning—before the kids wake up and before you shower and dress for work—is one way to prioritize writing. You also can block time before bed, but it can be easy to claim you are too tired to write at that point in the day. If you can commit to writing no matter what, then late-day writing works.

Habit # 5: Get Organized.

To write a book in a month, you need all your research, files, pens, sticky notes, etc., at your fingertips. You don't want to spend a ton of time regularly looking for what you need—even files you know you saved *somewhere* on your computer but now can't locate. If you do, you won't write; instead, you'll search.

You can use an online filing system, like Dropbox, Google Drive or Evernote, or an old-fashioned filing cabinet. It matters little if your "tools" are in the cloud or a box on top of your desk. Have everything you need handy and organized. That means you need to label folders and create a filing system that works for you—not for someone else.

Ingrain these habits in your writing life, and you can call on them not only during a 30-day writing event but at any time of the year. You'll find they make you more productive and help you achieve your writing goals consistently.

WRITING WITH SPEED
AND CRAFT

Two Trains for the Nonfiction Writing Track

By Roy Peter Clark

So you want to write a work of nonfiction and have 30 days to do it. How will you proceed? If I were in your shoes, I would think of the finished work as a destination and the process of writing as a journey. But what kind of journey? I could walk, but that might take too long. I could fly, but I might miss some stops along the way. I think I'll take a train.

If I choose to board a writing train, I still have to make an important decision: Will I take the Express or the Local?

The Express, we know, is quicker because it makes no stops along the way. The rider (or writer) settles in for a trip of a pre-determined duration and destination.

I prefer to write via the Express. It helps me feel the natural flow of good writing. To overcome writer's block, I just lower my standards and get my hands moving.

I draft as early as I can to take advantage of what I know and learn what I still need to know. I pay little attention to the requirements of the writing, knowing I will fulfill them along the way. I never procrastinate because even when my hands are not moving I'm rehearsing. This helps me anticipate problems and solve them in my head. It helps me predict what I need to do next. It disarms what Freud called "the watcher at the gate," that internal critic that stands in the way of creativity and experimentation.

That is my preferred method of travel, but, alas, the writing does not always cooperate.

Faced with obstacles, I will climb on board the Local. When I am riding the Local, I realize that there are stops along the way—points of departure where the parts of the writing process become more transparent and reliable. And those stops have names:

Idea Street

For me the first step in the writing process is the discovery of something worth writing about. With experience this becomes easier. Instead of saying, "I have nothing to write about," the writer learns to say, "I have three good story ideas. Which one will I choose?" The goal is to develop a level of curiosity that helps you see the world as a storehouse of story ideas.

Hunt Highway

Productive nonfiction writers don't just write with their hands; they also write with their legs. They get out of the office and engage the world. They find places where stories are happening. They meet people who have stories to tell. They are hunters and gatherers, collecting in their noteBooks the raw material that will bring the written work to life.

Focus Lane

Focus is the central act of the writing process, the ability to understand what the story is really about.

It begins with an effort to limit the topic, so that you are not writing about vandalism in American high schools, but in one school in St. Petersburg, Florida, that represents a larger reality. Focus—to use two metaphors—becomes both a door and a knife. As a door it lets in evidence to make your point. As a knife, it cuts out material not central to the reader's understanding.

Draft Boulevard

If you are having trouble drafting your story, you may have to get off the train and go back to an earlier stop, doing more work on the focus. That central idea is probably going to be expressed high in your story, either in a lead, a theme statement, or what is sometimes called the "nut paragraph." It will help you to begin drafting your story earlier than you think you can. If you begin drafting too late, you may run out of time, miss your deadline, or not reach your final stop.

Revision Way

Too many nonfiction writers spend too much of their time on the hunting and gathering. I've seen reporters work nine months on an investigation and then try to write it in less than nine hours. Early drafting leaves times for revision. It is during this final stage that some of the most important discoveries are made—in information, in language, and in meaning. So all aboard the writing train, my fellow writers. Take the Express if you can. But choose the Local if you must.

How to Write Nonfiction Fast and Well

By Roy Peter Clark

The secret to writing nonfiction fast and well is to write and report at the same time. This advice may sound either obvious or contradictory to some, but to me it has a Zen-like quality in which opposites are reconciled. What is the sound of two hands writing?

Good fast writing may seem like magic to those who bleed their words on the page or screen. But it is neither magic nor sanguinary. It is the result of a set of rational steps, a process that can be practiced and mastered.

The Process

It begins, of course, with the search for a story idea. It leads to a period of hunting and gathering, research and reporting that will create the raw material. Suddenly a focus emerges, a clearer sense of what the story is really about. That focus helps us select the best material we've collected. Somewhere along the way, an order comes into view, an architecture that helps us plan a beginning, middle, and ending. If these steps go well, then drafting should be a snap, leaving time for revision.

To describe writing this way seems mechanical and linear, I know, when it is really more organic and circular. If I can't figure out how to select the best material, I can go back a step and review the focus. If I have no focus yet, I turn back and collect more information. And, guess what, I can begin a draft at any time, even when I am just trying to discover a good idea. It may not be worthy of the name "first draft" yet. Maybe it's just a "zero draft" or "free draft" or "barf draft." But it gets my hands moving, my mind working, and it teaches me what I already know and what I have yet to learn.

Two Things that Slow You Down

Two things slow the writer, and we all have battled them: procrastination and writer's block. These are not identical evil twins, but they are first cousins. We experience both as negative forces that prove our unworthiness. Two great writing teachers from New Hampshire, Donald Murray and Donald Graves, taught me the antidotes to these poisons.

I no longer procrastinate. Now I rehearse. Anyone who has asked a boss for a raise knows how to rehearse, how to imagine a conversation long before you actually speak the words or pop the question. The time when I look like I am not writing, I am actually cooking the story in my mind—on one side of the brain or the other. This simmering on the stove lets me turn up the heat and deliver the meal in a timely and tasty way.

I never have writer's block. Now, on the advice of poet William Stafford, I just lower my standards—at the BEGINNING of the process. They can be raised as I move closer and closer to revision. I lower my standards by writing in pencil on a yellow pad, or blasting out 300 words on my computer, or writing myself or my editor a quick note about how the story is going.

When it comes to writing, I believe that struggle is over-rated. It may romanticize the craft, but that has never helped a writer please or instruct a single reader. In writing, and reading, the goal should be fluency and daily habit. "Remember," Donald Murray once told me, "a page a day equals a book a year."

The Key to Producing Good Work When Writing Quickly

By Lee Pound

How do you write quickly and write well at the same time? I've heard many people say it is impossible, that you must write and rewrite many times to produce good work.

However, many writers who have mastered their craft will tell you that good writing is a habit built up from experience. Many years ago, when I was a newspaper editor and reporter, I would return to the office at 11:30 at night with a mish-mash of notes and have to produce three front-page stories by midnight. I knew writers who could take hours to do this and still not produce good work. They didn't survive in the pressure world of newspapers. Deadlines are unforgiving.

Over the 15 years of pressure writing for newspapers, years of writing fiction, and years of editing and publishing nonfiction, I've learned a few powerful tips that will enable you to write quickly and well every time.

Make Decisions

The most important step is to make decisions. What is important and what isn't? Is anyone going to want to read it? Do I have enough information to write about this right now? Where do I start? Where do I end? How long is my story? What are the key points, and what can I leave out?

Many people can't decide what to write because they censor themselves. They toss out every idea that comes up from the subconscious and wait for a better one that never arrives because none of the ideas are good enough. Stop censoring if you want to write quickly.

8 Tips to Keep in Mind as You Write

I use the following tips with my clients and in everything I write. Some you will need to internalize with practice. Some you already are doing. All of them rely on you paying attention to your writing as you write. Be aware of what you write, be aware of the habitual words you use, and change them the next time they come up.

1. **Take a few minutes to plan out your writing.** Decide your major theme, decide where you will begin and where you will end, and jot down the three or four major topics you want to cover. This will eliminate several drafts and speed up the writing process because you have created a roadmap for your piece.

2. **Use the first sentence to grab the reader's attention.** This can be a question, bold statement, interesting fact, or some other item people want to know about. Raise a question the reader wants answered with this statement, and don't answer it until later.

3. **Train yourself to use the active voice as much as possible.** In most situations, this will strengthen your writing, because it will create a more forceful presence and direction. Your statements will be direct and firm.

4. **Vary the length of your sentences.** This will get rid of the staccato feel of a lot of short sentences running together at once. It also will create a comfortable rhythm for the reader.

5. **Don't use a lot of excess words.** Sentences filled with flab and unnecessary words slow down the reader and hide much of the

meaning of a sentence. Look for phrases beginning with "there is" and other such meaningless openers.

6. **Write shorter paragraphs.** This creates a more pleasing interface for your reader and an unconscious feeling that your piece is easier to read.

7. **End with a call to action of some kind.** Readers want you to tell them what to do with the information you have just given them. A call to action can be anything from a request to buy a product to implementing a process. Readers tend not to do anything if you don't give them guidance.

8. **After you finish your piece, read it over once, looking for each of these items.** Correct them and send it out.

There's More to Good Writing . . .

Good writing consists of more than just technical steps. Your content is important as well. If you have very little to say, your writing will have no effect no matter how well it is crafted.

Make certain your content is interesting to your readers. This piece is on writing and first appeared on a writing blog. Any other subject would be inappropriate. The blog was also about writing nonfiction, so I wouldn't want to write on how to create a novel. It wouldn't fit well.

Be a resource for your readers. We read because we want to know more about a given subject. We want tips that will help us do our work better. Provide information that your readers can use this instant.

Follow these tips to create good, fast writing that works both for you and for your readers.

Write Fast, on Point, and Nearly Perfectly in Your First Draft

By Nina Amir

When you know you have a deadline to meet, a real or a self-imposed one, it's important to find ways to move through writer's block and the desire to edit as you compose a first draft. That's the goal, of course—to write a first draft of something in 30 days. Some of you may actually get around to editing that first draft and producing a polished piece ready for submission or publishing during the Write Nonfiction in November Challenge. That's even better!

As a journalist, I often find myself under the pressure of deadlines. Additionally, as a blogger with four (yes, four) blogs, online columns, and regular guest post assignments, I have had to learn to write copy fast. I don't have time to dawdle over my articles or posts. I don't have time for writer's block. (What is writer's block?) And I don't have time to let my "Inner Critic" or "Inner Editor" take over while I'm composing. I only have time to write a rough draft fast. In fact, that rough draft can't even be too rough; in many cases, I have to get it close to right the first time. I may only have time for one round of editing.

How do I accomplish this feat day in and day out? Some techniques exist that help any writer, but especially nonfiction writers, write fast, on point, and as close to perfectly as possible every time (or almost every time) their hands hit the keyboard. Here are six I use regularly.

Six Tips for Writing Fast, on Point and Nearly Perfectly as You Compose Your First Draft

1. **Know what you want to write about.** This first tip is a bit like writing a pitch or elevator speech for a book. If you can summarize what you want to write about in 25 words or so, then you'll be able to sit down and write about it without beating around the bush at the beginning. A good summary statement allows you to lead into that statement and then out of it with targeted points pretty quickly. Most nonfiction requires exactly that: a statement of purpose and follow-up points. You might want to add in some nice anecdotes or stories to illustrate your points, but that's easy once you have the basic outline. So, start by figuring out exactly what you want to write about, and then let your e-book or book flow out of that. Break a longer project into smaller pieces in the same manner; write smaller summary statements or pitches for each chapter or each section of a chapter.

2. **Have a Structure:** The first tip assumes you have a structure for your book. If you don't already have one, be sure you create one before you start. The process in step one will help you create a detailed table of contents, or outline, to follow so you never wonder what you need to write next.

3. **Write Fast:** Write the sections of your book in short bursts or periods of time. Studies show we work better in shorter increments, such as 15 or 30 minutes. Use a timer, and try timed writings. Write as fast as you can for 15, 30, 45, or 60 minutes. Then take a break. Reward yourself with a snack, a cup of tea, a walk around the block, a cat-petting session, or 10 minutes of yoga. Then set the timer and start again. You'll be amazed at how much writing you can get done this way and how quickly you can get in the flow each time the "writing sprint" begins. You can actually find writing sprint partners on Twitter by searching #writingsprint. There is no need to sit down for two hours or more at a time to knock out the amount

of writing you need to produce or to meet a deadline. This can produce writer's block, and the monotony of sitting for so long also can make you write more slowly or cause you to become distracted and tired. Writing in short bursts is more effective because you remain more present.

4. **Don't allow your Inner Editor or Inner Critic to join you.** Most writers like to revise as they write. That's your Inner Critic or Inner Editor at work. When you feel the pressure of a deadline, however, these inner colleagues only slow you down. Picking apart every sentence or word makes writing a tedious and time-consuming process. Going back over a whole section or several pages to improve grammar and syntax can mean 30 minutes of precious time when you could have been writing two more pages of copy. Tell your Inner Editor to wait! His or her time will come—and soon enough. When the first draft has been completed, the Inner Editor's role becomes extremely important. That's when the two of you team up to begin the job of polishing your manuscript. You want your Inner Editor working hard then; you need an Inner Critic—a really critical eye—at that point but not before, especially if you are trying to knock out a book in a month. Until that time, ask your "Inner Skilled Writer" to join you as you whip out that first draft. He or she knows how to construct a strong sentence and where to put the commas and semicolons. If the changes can be made quickly, make them. Just don't pore over your copy. Keep writing with confidence, and keep in mind that a first draft does not have to be perfect, just finished!

5. **Set small word-count goals.** Setting out to write 1,500 words per day can feel overwhelming. Instead, try writing 500 words per day, or 500 words three times perday. This number of words equates to one blog posts, which feels much more "doable" than a whole chapter, for example. That's why blogging a book, works so well; each "installment" is only about 300 to 500 words. You can use this strategy in conjunction with writing

sprints. Set a word count and try to meet it in a certain amount of time. For example, tell yourself you'll write 500 words in 20 minutes.

6. **Avoid distractions.** Nothing will create errors in your writing and slow your progress more consistently than distractions, and today writers are faced with more distractions than ever before. To write a book in a month, plan to cut down on distractions. Utilize some of the online programs that stop you from accessing the internet, or create an environment in your home that is conducive to focusing on your project. For more information on the tools you might utilize to accomplish this, read this post.

Of course, everyone's writing needs a bit of editing and polishing. No first draft is a final draft, but some come pretty darn close. First you have to get that draft written, though. Hopefully, these tips will help get you moving all year long but especially during the next 30 days as you take the nonfiction writing challenge.

How to Speak Your Book

By Nina Amir

Many people don't believe they are writers. However, they want to become authors. This leaves them in a quandary. They want and maybe need a book but don't feel they can write it.

Others are in a hurry and don't have the time to write, even though they know they can.

If you are one of these aspiring authors, stop stressing! If you can speak, you can write—and fast. You can even speak your book. In fact, you can speak it in a month. How is that possible? Simple.

5 Steps to Speak Your Book

Here's a methodology for speaking a book that I use successfully with my clients who aren't comfortable writing or who want to get their book written fast. This method is easy, quick, and more affordable than hiring a ghostwriter. Plus, it produces a book filled with their own knowledge and experience offered in their own voice.

If you need to speak, rather than write, your book to get it done in a month—or just want to try this method, here are the exact steps I use with my clients to get their books out of their heads and onto paper—without them hardly typing a word.

1. **Mind map the idea.** Start by brainstorming the book idea. You may have only a general topic, but work until you fine-

tune this to a subject and an angle. End up with a table of contents—a list of topics you will cover in each chapter. This provides you with the basic structure for the book.

2. **Create a detailed table of contents.** Continue brainstorming, or mind mapping, until you have more content than just chapter titles or subjects. Then, take the smaller subjects you thought of during the mind mapping process and place them in your table of contents under the appropriate chapter. These could be used as subheadings in your chapters, and if you wish, you can set them up as such in your table of contents. Also, create bullet points under each subheading to remind you of the topics you want to discuss. Take the time to make notes, if necessary, on each chapter, subheading, bullet point, or topic so you feel sure you know what you want to say for each one. The point is to get as detailed as possible (without writing the book). Imagine this like a PowerPoint presentation; you need enough information so you spark your memory and you know what to say, but you don't necessarily want to write everything out in sentences and paragraphs.

3. **Speak your book chapter by chapter.** Using the detailed table of contents, speak your book into a digital recorder. You also can use a free teleseminar line.

4. **Get your recordings transcribed.** Hire a transcriptionist to take your audio recordings and turn them into a Word document. Or use Word's dictation system or a program like Dragon Naturally Speaking as you record your book during the previous step. This avoids the cost of transcription.

5. **Edit your transcripts.** Tackle your manuscript once yourself before hiring an editor. This saves you money. It also gives you the chance to ensure what you said made sense. (Often what we say is unintelligible.) Once you've done this, send it to a professional book editor for a round or two (or three) of developmental editing and then a round of line editing.

Bonus tip: If step #3, speaking your book chapter by chapter, feels awkward to you, turn your detailed table of contents into questions. Then have someone interview you. Record your answers with a voice recorder (or use a teleseminar line), and follow the rest of the steps.

To do this in a month, create a schedule. If you have 12 chapters, then you need about 12 hours to speak each of those chapters—possibly less if they are short. With four weeks, that means you need just three hours per week to get your book spoken.

Leave time for a transcriptionist to do his or her magic; maybe one chapter could be transcribed per week. Then you give yourself a few hours per chapter for editing and revising.

Voila! You have a full manuscript.

How much further editing that document still needs will vary, but if you've planned out your book in fine detail—the more detail the better—and stuck to that detail as you spoke your book, it should be in pretty good shape. You also need to have created a sound book structure in those early stages. If you didn't, a developmental editor will find many reasons to move content around and make other major changes.

Once editing is complete, your book is ready for design and proofreading. Then you can publish and start boosting your business as an author as well as an entrepreneur.

Three Techniques to Help You Write a Book in a Month

By Jay Artale

All write-a-book-in-a-month events help you move quickly and effectively through tasks that allow you to achieve your goal—a completed first draft. And they put you in the writing flow.

Too many writers agonize over a first draft for years, and many overthink and become perfectionistic about their projects. As a result, they don't get around to writing one word of the manuscript, let alone a complete manuscript in a month. However, when you set a target of writing a book within a limited period—like 30 days—you increase the sense of urgency. The deadline pushes you to act rather than get stuck at the preparation stage or in perfectionism.

The urgency created by such a tight deadline necessitates writing faster than usual and increasing your level of focus. Therefore, when you sit down to write, you put all your attention on writing and perform this task with an eye on the clock. After all, you have a deadline to meet! Your focus and urgency trigger your subconscious mind, which puts you in the flow or zone. That's when writing becomes magically easy.

To help you make the most of the opportunity provided by the WNFIN Challenge, try the following three strategies. Each will help you successfully write a book in a month.

Get into the Zone

When you write quickly, you bypass your conscious mind and analytical thought processes and tap into the wealth of information nestled within your subconscious mind. If you've ever found yourself in the writing zone, you know the experience. Words fly from your mind to the screen or paper so fast you can hardly type or write fast enough to record them. The words flow because you are tapped into your subconscious mind.

The subconscious mind absorbs ideas and information that bypass your conscious mind entirely. Therefore, during a 30-day writing challenge, you want to do whatever possible to tap into your subconscious when you write. If you haven't already tried freewriting to get you into the writing zone, it's worth experimenting with at the start of November.

Freewriting involves writing with an imposed time limit without thinking about *what* you are writing during that period. You write as quickly as you can and resist revising, editing, spell-checking, or researching during that period.

Since freewriting creates urgency, this tactic helps you mentally get out of your way and access the wealth of content buried deep within your mind. You write in the moment—no time to allow your mind to wander to the past or future, and, as a result, easily tap into your unconscious information reserve.

Write Every Day

With only 30 days available to complete your writing project, meeting this challenge successfully requires using every one of them to build and maintain your momentum. Even if you only write a few sentences or paragraphs on some days, this is better than skipping a day entirely.

Skipping one day of writing is like standing at the top of a slippery slope. This one day provides you with the excuse to miss another... then another. Before you know it, a week will have passed, and you'll find it easier to give up than try and make up for lost writing time. You'll have slid to the bottom of the mountain.

If time is not the issue and, instead, you don't feel like writing some days or feel your inspiration has dried up, commit to writing for 15 minutes. Half the writing battle is just showing up ready and willing to fight for what's important to you—writing your book. Show up in your writing space with the identity and mindset of *I am a writer; therefore, I write.* Then, you'll be amazed at how easy it becomes to over-deliver on that solitary paragraph or 15-minutes writing commitment you made to yourself.

Additionally, if you write every day in November, you'll develop a daily writing habit. That habit will keep your writing momentum going this month and beyond. You stop wondering *if* you will write today and know that you sit down and write daily because...well...it's your habit to do so.

Let Go of Perfection

As writers, we often put too much pressure on ourselves to achieve perfection when writing a book. Remember, during the WNFIN Challenge, you're not writing the final draft; you're writing the first draft. As a result, the manuscript you produce during November may be peppered with errors, bad grammar, spelling mistakes, and redundancies. Some of the content will be so bad that you'll cut it and drag it into the trash.

Give yourself permission to write badly. If you're a perfectionist, this is a tough ask, but it's a good habit to get into if you want to complete a first draft within 30 days. To accomplish though, you'll need to be aware when your Inner Critic begins weighing in on what you're writing.

I vividly remember writing the first draft of my first book. I agonized over sentence and paragraph structure, and that draft took more than six months to complete. By the time it was written, I was fatigued by reviewing and re-reading my content. When it came to self-editing the completed draft, I almost gave up. Avoid this scenario by barging through your first draft at breakneck speed.

There's a bonus to this approach. Not only do you finish your first draft in a month but, when you reread it during the self-editing phase, it will seem like you are reading it for the first time. Seeing your work with fresh eyes is imperative if you want to revise and edit well.

Don't Edit While You Write

I love this quote by author Jodi Picoult: *"You might not write well every day, but you can always edit a bad page. You can't edit a blank page."*

Look at writing and editing as two distinctly different phases, and during November, only focus on writing.

Editing as you write your first draft is a big no-no. It's a sure-fire way to ask your Inner Critic to participate in the writing process, which slows you down considerably. Plus, it's a procrastination technique that keeps you from drafting the next sentence. It anchors you to a spot in your manuscript, so you can avoid writing something new.

While you will eventually want to utilize proven editing techniques, wait until December to start revising. Right now, focus on productivity while challenging yourself to let go of any desire to edit or revise. Here are a few editing traps to skirt during the WNFIN Challenge:

- **Avoid reviewing your paragraphs during your writing session.** Your writing sessions are for writing, not for reading. Avoid the temptation to write a sentence or paragraph and keep re-reading it to make it perfect. Now is *not* the time to tease your rough first draft paragraphs into a thing of beauty.

- **Stop fixing spell mistakes.** Don't get distracted and search for the correct spelling. If you have your writing program set to alert you to every spelling or grammar error, turn it off. Those red or underlined words will become distractions. You'll need a steel will to avoid fixing them on the spot.

- **Don't search for the perfect word.** You will get pulled out of the writing zone when you can't think of the right word for a sentence and search for it. Rather than continuing to write, you may pause to encourage it to appear in your conscious mind. Often, I think of a similar word, but not the one I want. That's when I'll open an online thesaurus and search for the word. While this gets the right word inserted, it breaks my subconscious stream of content and makes it difficult to get back into the writing zone. Plus, it wastes writing time. If you can think of a similar word, but you know it's not the right one, put () around the word, e.g., *(delicate),* or add text that is easy to find in a document search, e.g., *delicateXX* or *(synonym).* You can type these cues without breaking your flow. If you can't think of the word you want to add, you also can simply add XX or __ in its place. Then address these missing words in the first round of self-editing.

Writing a first draft—messy or neat—should be your November goal. To accomplish it, *write fast. Full steam ahead. Don't spare the horses...* and any other idiom that motivates you to write quickly.

Can you imagine having a finished first draft to polish at the end of 30 days? How good with that feel? Your sense of achievement will be immense. There's no time to waste—Let's write!

Six Scary Good Tricks to Help You Write a Book in a Month

By Nina Amir

Halloween takes place right before the start of November writing challenges. It's a time to take the kids trick or treating, dress up for your friend's party, and cue up *The Night of the Living Dead*. But when you wake up tomorrow morning with a sugar hangover, you'll wish you'd spent some time accumulating tricks and treats to help you tackle your book-in-a-month project.

If you are reading this on October 31 or November 1, it not too late to plan some tricks and use them (and also get treats) to start and finish a nonfiction project in 30 days successfully.

To increase the likelihood of succeeding at a 30-day writing challenge, you need six scary good tricks that come directly from the world of Certified High Performance Coaching. Specifically, you want these high-performance habits in your bag of nonfiction writing tricks. If you have—and use—them during a book-in-a-month event, you'll finishing that event successfully. In fact, you'll deem them treats worth drooling over.

Trick #1: Seek Clarity

When you habitually seek clarity, you consistently feel engaged in and fulfilled by your writing project. The clearer you are about your book-in-a-month project, the higher the likelihood that you will get from start to finish.

Clarity during a 30-day writing challenge ensures you don't start and stop because you begin doubting that the project is headed in the correct direction. When you feel clear, you don't wonder if you are the right person to write the book.

Instead, you feel bold and enthusiastic about writing. Your confidence in yourself and the project keep your energy high and your focus on the goal. That means you write consistently.

If you aren't sure you have enough clarity about your book project to succeed at the challenge, ask yourself questions like:

- Who are my readers?
- Why did I feel compelled to write this in the first place?
- Who needs this book?
- How can I best share what I know with my audience?

Your answers will provide the clarity you need.

Trick #2: Generate Energy

Many writers fail at the Write Nonfiction in November Challenge merely because they lack the energy to succeed. Those who write productively and enthusiastically for 30 days, have generated the trifecta of energy: emotional, mental, and physical.

You need all three types of energy to remain high until you finish the challenge. That prevents you from quitting partway through because your energy became depleted in one or more of these areas.

Energy keeps your stamina, motivation, and passion high so you can write daily...for a month. High-Performance studies show that energy is one of the most significant predictors of productivity.

When taking on a 30-day writing event, however, many writers end up stressed. And stress is a huge energy zapper.

To avoid this problem and maintain high energy during WNFIN, keep up an exercise routine during November (even if it's just walking for 30 minutes daily), eat a healthy diet (no Halloween candy allowed!), sleep seven to eight hours per night, and be sure to drink a lot of water and breathe deeply. Try taking a break every hour to stretch, breathe, and hydrate. You'll be amazed at how high your energy will stay if you implement this one trick.

Trick #3: Raise Necessity

You must have a good reason to write a book in a month. You must feel it's *necessary* to complete that nonfiction project in 30 days. And your sense of *necessity* leads you to consistent action—in this case, daily writing.

Do you feel you *must* write your book—like doing so is the only option? Do you have a clear sense that people need your book *now* and so you *must* write it for them? If you answer "yes" to those questions, you've raised your necessity.

If not, get in touch with your Big Why for writing your book. What's the reason you want to write it? When you know that…and connect with a sense of urgency to get it written…you'll have little trouble writing every day and completing your project by the end of the 30 days.

Trick #4: Increase Productivity

Of course, to write a book in a month, you must be productive. But many writers are not because they don't set goals and remain focused as they work toward them.

You're lucky! You've got a goal: write a book in a month. You've even got a deadline to increase your urgency a bit—finish 30 days from when you begin. Yet, you still need to develop a strategy to stay focused for an entire month on completing your project.

Of course, in our fast-paced and digital world, it's important to plan how you will reduce distractions. That means you need to know what steals your focus in the first place.

Are you most distracted by email, social media, your children, the dogs, the mess in your office, the laundry that needs to get done, your boss' requests, or friends asking you to go to lunch? Whatever "focus thief" shows up in your life most often must be put on notice...now...to leave you alone in November (or during whatever month you choose to write your book).

That could mean that you tell everyone you won't be reading or answering email until 10 a.m. during the coming month. Why? Because you'll be writing first thing in the morning. (When you stop reading email first thing in the morning you increase your productivity significantly.) Or it might mean turning off your phone and the internet for two hours each day. It also could mean recording all your favorite shows so you can watch them after you write...or the month after you complete your book. Perhaps it means getting another mom to agree to watch your kids five days a week for an hour (while you write).

Add clarity, energy and necessity, to your plan to reduce distractions, and you'll find your productivity skyrocketing.

Trick #5: Develop Influence

What's the trick to influence? First, persuade yourself to write daily—to stick to your writing schedule. Also, influence yourself to carry out your productivity plan and energy strategies. Then, you need to ask for what you want and need—support for achieving your goal of completing a book in a month.

You also need to influence yourself to say "no" more often, especially for the next 30 days. Say "yes" to writing daily, and "no" to that last minute volunteer project, the unpaid (or paid) talk that requires a two-hour drive to the venue, and the three-hour hike with your friends.

Influence is the ability to shape other people's behavior, too. You want to motivate them to help you achieve your goal. As mentioned, that might mean asking them to do something for you, like walk the dogs.

To motivate people to do what you ask, tell them about your dream. Then ask them about theirs. How can helping you achieve your dream get them closer to realizing an aspiration of their own? Getting them excited about achieving their goals can make them want to help you do the same.

Trick #6: Demonstrate Courage

Writers need courage. It takes bold action to put your words on paper and share them with others.

Additionally, you must courageously make whatever changes are necessary to ensure you complete the 30-day writing challenge. That means you need the courage to change yourself.

You might feel the need to be courageous when telling your partner you will be doing less laundry, cooking, and childcare while you write a book in a month. You may need a bit of courage to tell your friends about your goal and to ask them to hold you accountable. You may feel the need for courage to change your sleeping habits and get up at 5 a.m. to ensure you get your writing in before you head to your "real job."

Sharing what you know or your life experiences definitely can feel courageous as well. It's a bit like facing your demons and then letting the world get to know them, too.

But high-performance writers are courageous people, and that makes them more productive as well. They boldly say "no" and shut their door to all sorts of opportunities and people to ensure they do what's most important to them. And, you know what? That makes them happier as well.

Tricks Get Results

You are now armed with six tricks to help you increase your performance during your 30-day writing challenge. If you use them, you are sure to get some awesome treats—the results you set out to achieve.

What are they? Oh! Sweet things writers enjoy most, like seeing a pile of typed pages growing on your desk, feeling the satisfaction of a productive writing period, knowing you finished a manuscript, realizing you do have something important to say—and you said it on paper, and completing what you set out to do.

Maybe the sweetest treat of all, though, is knowing you can write consistently, quickly, and productively, which means you are a writer.

FAST NONFICTION
BOOK STRUCTURES

How to Write a Short Book Fast

By Nina Amir

In my work coaching writers, I have discovered a primary reason why aspiring authors don't follow through and become published authors: the thought of writing and publishing a 150-250 page book (or 35,000 to 50,000 words) sends them into overwhelm and feelings of inadequacy. When that happens, they freeze up and don't write a single word.

If you plan to take on the challenge of writing a book in a month, and you suffer from the limiting belief that you can't write a long book, you'll struggle through your 30-day writing event. Instead of tackling a long book—or your "big" book project, take the same approach I offer to my clients: Write a short book.

Short books can be anywhere from 16 to 100 pages in length (or 2,500 to 30,000 words). That's much more manageable. I'm not talking about your magnum opus. This is, indeed, a short book and therefore much less intimidating to produce. Plus, it can be written quickly—in 30 days or even less.

The 10 Short Nonfiction Book Structures

I can think of 10 types of short book structures that lend themselves to writing a book in a month, some of which Rochelle Melander also describes in _Write-A-Thon: Write Your Book in 26 Days (And Live to Tell about It)_. You easily can turn these formats into printed books (saddle stitched, spiral bound, or perfect bound) or e-books.

1. Tip Book

A tip book usually provides 10-101 tips on a certain subject. Normally, one tip is highlighted per page, but some tip books offer many per page. In the latter case, the book consists of just one long list of tips. Each tip might be just a sentence long, or you can include a paragraph or two of explanation per tip. This determines how many you include on the page and how long the book becomes.

To write a tip book in a month, first compose a list of tips about something you know a lot about, that you want to teach, or that your potential readers ask you about frequently. This could be 30 tips for playing better golf—and you write one tip per day—or 101 tips on how to increase your income in a month—and you write approximately four tips per day during your write-a-book-in-a-month challenge.

2. List Book

If you are like most people, you write lists all the time. That means you can write a list book. This book structure consists of a list of 10-101 things your readers need to know on a particular subject. To start, compile the list. Then, write a short, informative essay to go with each item on your list. Or just write a list and publish it. Determine how many items will be on your list, and then calculate how many writing sessions or days you require to write the short book.

3. Quotation Book

Inspirational books based on quotations and a theme can prove a quick, easy writing project. Start with an epigraph, a quote at the beginning of your chapter, and then write a short essay to go with it. Or use quotations of your own—or from your books. This type of book requires research to locate the quotations, but you can compose the rest of the content off the top of your head and share your own expertise, thoughts, and experiences.

4. Rx Book

Prescriptive nonfiction can be written in short form using a variety of formats. Provide guidance or direction—a prescription for what ails your readers—on a particular topic. This could be 10 steps for better relationships, 12 ways to build your business, or a guide to indoor gardening, for example. You could be the expert author, or you could interview experts and include their information. Any how-to subject can be turned into an "Rx" book. Just solve a problem, answer a question, or ease someone's pain.

To write such a book, jot down the steps, rules, or ways—your basic how-to information, and begin writing your advice. Once you know how many steps you have in your "process," you can determine how many writing sessions you need. If you have seven steps or ten ways, you will need seven or ten sessions to write the book (plus two more for an introduction and a conclusion).

5. Anthology

This book structure could require a bit of pre-planning to get contributors on board. For an anthology, you solicit content from other experts. You may also write a little—an introduction and conclusion and possibly a piece of your own.

To produce an anthology, also called a compilation, ask 10-25 experts each to contribute a chapter to your book. (Again, these could be guest blog posts.) All the chapters, or contributions, should relate to one topic; in fact, plan out the content for the book, then ask the appropriate experts to contribute to your book. Give each of them a topic and details on what you expect from them.

6. One-Concept Book

Do you have a "big idea" you'd love to get across to readers or to the world at large—a concept you think would catapult you and your business to success? That idea could be perfect for a short book. To write a one-concept book, introduce your idea, and then explain it in a concise fashion. Explore it further using anecdotes, case studies, reports, research, statistics, and any other evidence, including your own experience. Think of your book as one long chapter broken down into subheadings. You might include an introduction and conclusion. It might end up reading like a manifesto or a long article. This makes it even less intimidating to some people. Determine how long you think your one-concept book will be by making a list of the main points you want to make. If you have 10 points to make, you probably need about 12 days to write the book. You need at least one or two days to write the first piece that describes your big idea.

7. Q & A Book

A question and answer book is structured just the way it sounds: Each chapter is a question, and the content of that chapter provides the answer. To write this type of book, make a list of your potential readers' most common questions. If you have 30 questions, you'll need to answer at least one per day. If you have fewer questions, you can probably take some days off. Add an introductory chapter, but include an extra writing session to finish that as well.

8. Benefit Book

Structured much like a Q & A book, a benefit book discusses the benefits of something, such as a particular diet, a way to exercise, or blogging. You could have five benefits or 1001. It's up to you. For each one, you write a short essay (or even just a paragraph or two) describing the benefit. To complete a book with 20 benefits, you should need just 20 days. If it has an intro and a conclusion, add two more days to your writing schedule.

9. Problem/Solution Book

Similar to the previous two book structures, a problem/solution book revolves around providing solutions to common problems in a particular subject area. If you know your potential readers' most common or pressing questions, write them down. Then set out to answer them as you create your manuscript. If, for example, you have 10 questions, you will need ten sessions or days to write up the answers. Again, add on one to three days to compose an introduction and a conclusion.

10. Essay Book

An essay book is comprised of a number of your essays on one topic or on related topics. You could, for instance, decide to write a book with 30 essays on motherhood, jogging, or gardening. If you write one a day, you'll be done in a month. You might want to add an introduction, of course.

Tips for Writing a Short Book Fast

Here are two additional tips to keep in mind as you write a short book fast:

- To write a short book fast you need to plan out your content. Each one of the structures above allows you to almost "fill in the blanks" with your content ideas.

- Work smarter, not harder. Keep your chapters short. Most of the nonfiction book structures mentioned above lend themselves to doing so. Keep track of your word count so you don't write more than necessary.

You also can complete a book quickly by repurposing material. Consider compiling old articles or essays on one topic, blog posts written in a series (or on one topic), or any other bits and pieces of material you've previously written. Drop it into any one of the formats mentioned above.

By employing one of these ten short-book structures, you'll write your book fast. In the process, you'll build your confidence for writing that "big" book. Or you might decide you like writing short books and end up knocking out several a year.

Writing Booklets vs. Books

By Nina Amir

A short book constitutes a super choice for a book-in-a-month project, and today you can not only write but also publish such a book in a variety of ways in 30 days or less. Although you might gravitate toward producing a short e-book, consider a booklet instead. Later you can turn it into an e-book if you wish, possibly even within the constraints of your one-month deadline. But your booklet will afford you the benefit of having a physical book to sell and to hand to people.

I came upon this form of nonfiction writing when a friend of mine shared with me what she had learned in a class about promotion for speakers and writers. The man who taught the class suggested that speakers and writers should have something to sell at the back of the room when they appeared for an event, and he suggested selling booklets. These short (often only 28-pages) printed books can be produced at your local print shop since they are simply copied, stapled, and folded. (Some print shops have booklet presses, which makes production faster and cheaper.) This man's version didn't even involve a professionally designed color cover, just use of a colored cover stock.

Short Versions of Your "Big" Book

I produced one of these when I got frustrated by my inability to get one of my book projects sold to a publisher. I pulled one section of the book-to-be out of the manuscript and published it as a booklet, which

I called *From Empty Practice to Meaning-Full and Spirit-Full Prayers and Rituals . . . In 7 Simple Steps*. Unwilling to wait for a publisher to pick up another book project about which I felt quite passionate, I produced a second booklet, *The Kabbalah of Conscious Creation, 10 Mystical Steps to Manifesting Your Dreams and Desires*. I went on to produce two more booklets based on "big" book projects as well, *The Priestess Practice: 4 Steps to Creating Sacred Space and Inviting the Divine to Dwell Within It* and <u>*Navigating the Narrow Bridge: 7 Steps for Moving Forward Courageously Even When the Life Seems Most Precarious*</u>. The latter book I eventually made into an e-book and uploaded it to Amazon's Kindle Direct Publishing (KDP) platform; the others have been turned into PDFs, which I sell as e-books from <u>my website</u>.

The Benefits of Booklets

I like this form of publication for several reasons.

1. **I can revise my booklets as often as I like.** I don't publish many of them at a time, so if I want to make changes, it's no problem. I make the changes on my computer and then run a disc down to FedEx Kinko's or Office Depot. The next day, I have new booklets. One of them, *Abracadabra!*, has already grown by eight pages, and I'm about to revise it once again. When I'm done, it will have grown by at least another eight pages. One day it will be large enough for me to self-publish in another form, but in the meantime I can continue selling it when I speak and on my website, which allows me to promote prior the book being complete. It also allows me to test market the idea. The more sales of the booklet, the more proof I have for a publisher that the idea will fly as a full-length book.

2. **People prefer to read short books.** A booklet simply is a short book—a quick and easy read. With the busy lifestyle most of us have today, this form appeals to many people. In fact, I recently saw a series of booklets on sale in a bookstore. They

were short and simple with no spine—just copied and stapled, or saddle stitched. (And they were self-published.) The fact that a major store carried them and featured them at the check-out counter convinced me that production and sales of booklets was a viable publishing option. I've since seen this same series of booklets in some smaller bookstores.

3. **Booklets provide a quick and easy structure for producing a book.** I can take an idea I have for a full-length book and write it in booklet form in just a week or two. I then have a product to sell. People get to read what I've written, and I get to sell my booklet. In the process, that booklet helps me promote the book I ultimately want to sell to a publisher. That booklet also helps me show a publisher how I would deal with the subject I am proposing and that I am serious about helping promote and market my book project.

4. **Should my book project never get traditionally published, I've not waited around so long that I've lost interest in ever writing about that subject.** I've produced a nonfiction book that I have self-published, that people can read, and from which I can earn a bit of money. In fact, I've earned quite a bit of money at the back of the room after giving a speech or workshop. Booklets cost only a few dollars to produce, and I sell them for $5 to $10 a piece.

5. **I can produce booklets from repurposed material or from scratch.** Most of my booklets were produced from information I had written for my "big" books. I condensed, rewrote, and added some material as well. One was created from transcripts of a four-part teleseminar series I offered based on several chapters in a book I planned to write. I know someone who produced an e-book every few weeks from repurposed material, but you could also produce a booklet; if you have enough pages, you could produce a print-on-demand version, too. All that said, you can, of course, write from scratch.

6. **You don't have to worry about the chicken-before-the-egg issue when you speak to build author platform.** With my booklets in hand, prior to having a "real" published book, when I would go speak somewhere, I had my booklets to sell at the back of the room like all good writers—I mean speakers—should have. And this qualified me as an "author," which got me more speaking gigs.

Booklet Structure for a Tip Book

A tip book is possibly the easiest booklet to produce from scratch in 30 days. These 16 steps will help you format and write a tip book with 10 tips and 36 pages including the cover (Use the same basic format for more or fewer tips):

1. **Create a list of tips solving 10 problems.** Title this list, and your book, something like, "How to A so You Can B" Or "10 Tips on How to C." You can also make these "steps" or "ways."

2. **Devote two pages of your actual design (back and front) to each tip.** Your booklet will be 5.5" x 8.5" (8.5" x 11" folded in half). The top of the page includes the tip number, and the bottom has the copy, which may extend to the back of the page. If it does not, you can put a quotation or art on the back of the page.

3. **Put the book title and your name on the front cover.** The inside front cover remains blank. (That constitutes 2 pages.) Drop art onto the cover if you want. (I had professional cover designs created for most of mine.)

4. **Next, repeat the front cover page.** This is the title page and becomes page #1 (but it will not have a number in the footer).

5. **On the back of the title page, you can have a blank page.** This is page #2, but it won't have a page number.

6. **Now add your copyright page.** This is unnumbered page #3. (Model the information from any book.)

7. **On the back of page #3 is a blank page (unnumbered page #4).** Or you can place a quote or a graphic here.

8. **On page #5-6, place an introduction to your book.** Typically, this is numbered page #1.

9. **On pages #7-26, place your 10 tips on the front and (if necessary) back of each page.** You can place a quotation on any empty page.

10. **Your "About the Author" page is placed on page #27.** Place a blank page on the other side, page #28, unless your bio extends that far.

11. **On page #29, include testimonials about you or your work.**

12. **On page #30, include a quote or graphic (or a blank page).**

13. **Page #31 can be for promotional material,** like an order form or info about other products, booklets, seminars, or talks you offer.

14. **Page #32 remains blank.**

15. **Finally, page #33, is the inside cover, which remains blank and has no page number.** And then the back cover, #34, is where you can put promotional copy or simply your company name, contact info, and the price of the book near the bottom of the cover, or treat it like the back of any book and create back-cover copy.

16. **Create a PDF of continuous single pages if you are using a booklet press or any normal laser printer.** (If you are using a printing press or POD printer of some sort, your cover file may need to be a "spread.")

If you add or subtract pages and you print on a laser or booklet printer, your pages must be in multiples of 4. If you print on any other type of press, you need multiples of 2. Keep in mind that you might need the booklet trimmed (cut) along the edge, so design with extra space along the outside edge of the book.

You can use this tip-book structure to create any type of booklet. Here's the basic structure I used for most of mine, which produces a 36-40 page booklet:

1. Create a front and back cover with blank pages on the reverse side (4 pages).

2. Create a title page and a copyright page with blank pages on the reverse side (4 pages).

3. Write a two-page introduction.

4. Write four pages on each of 3-4 topics (12-16 pages).

5. Add 2-4 tips or tools, each 1-2 pages. These can be back-to-back, and if you have a blank page fill it with a quotation (2-6 pages).

6. Add a conclusion (1-2 pages).

7. And an "About the Author" page (1-2 pages with a blank page if only one page long).

8. Add in a page with information on how to contact you. This gets a blank page on the reverse side if you don't fill it.

9. Add another page with any other books or products you have. Again, if you don't use the reverse side, it remains blank.

You are now ready to write a booklet in a month. You even can get really motivated and turn it into an e-book and a POD book as well.

How to Structure a Nonfiction Book for a 30-Day Challenge

By Nina Amir

You've got an idea for a nonfiction book, and you want to write it in 30 days. You've brainstormed ideas for content, completed a mind map, or come up with a tentative outline. Now you need to determine how to structure your book in a way that will allow you to write your book quickly.

It's not that difficult to create a structure for a nonfiction book. Although not all nonfiction books follow the same structure, if you spend time looking at a variety of them, you will discover their basic format is pretty similar. In particular, if you look at books in the same niche or category as the one you want to write, you'll see that many of them follow the same basic format.

Find a Model

That's why one of the easiest ways to create a structure for your nonfiction book involves studying the bestselling books in the category in which your book will be sold. You also can find books in that category that you like and study them. Make note of the similarities in structure, such as how many chapters they have, if they have forewords, introductions, and conclusions, if they contain any special features, or if they use research, anecdotes, or personal experiences. Also pay attention to the tense used. Are they written in the first or third person? Then copy that structure and style as you design and write your own book.

Stick with the Basics

If you don't want to look at what other people have done, stick with the basics. The majority of nonfiction books have between 10 and 15 chapters. Each has a title that indicates what the chapter is about. The chapters are broken down into sections with appropriate subheadings or subtitles, which also clearly tell the reader what information they can find in each one.

The majority of nonfiction books also include an introduction and a conclusion.

Book titles, subtitles, chapter titles, and subheadings in chapters all tend to state the topic at hand, and these days they also use keywords, or search terms.

Consider Adding Special Features

Many nonfiction books have special features. These might be epigraphs, or quotes at the beginning of each chapter. Or you could mix it up and place a quote at the end of the chapter. Some nonfiction books include exercises or tips or have a workbook element. Yours could even include case studies or success stories set apart in some way that makes them appear "special."

Front Matter and Back Matter

Every book should have front matter: a copyright page, a dedication, and acknowledgements. Back matter consists of your author bio, information on your other books (if you have any), your products or services or company, or even a free offer that drives readers to your website to sign up for your mailing list. It also might include an index or bibliography.

Mind Map First vs. Structure First

Once you decide upon the basic structure of your book, you should find it fairly simple to drop your content into it, especially if you conduct a mind mapping exercise to develop the content of your book prior to this. Some writers like to brainstorm with a mind map (or in some other way) first and let the content dictate the structure of the book. This often works extremely well. However, you also can decide on the structure for the book and then mind map your book with the structure in mind. You may find this helps you visualize the book as you brainstorm content; then drop your ideas into the structure you've created.

With the structure of your book planned out, as well as the content, you are ready to write your book fast!

How to Blog a Book
or Book a Blog

By Nina Amir

Most writers don't seem to want to explore the world of blogging. They see it as just one more thing to do. They don't realize that blogging affords them a superb way to promote themselves and their work and to write a book quickly at the same time.

I don't know of any better way for writers to get a book written quickly while promoting their work and building author platform than by blogging a book. In fact, blogging is one of the most effective ways to accomplish these tasks and to get noticed by agents and acquisitions editors in the process. Today, just as many—if not more—bloggers are landing blog-to-book deals as in 2009, which reportedly was the height of the blog-to-book trend.

A successful blog acts like a beacon to publishers looking for the closest thing they can find to a test-marketed book idea and to a vetted writer—one they feel they can count on to bring in readers, by which I mean book buyers. If you actually blog your book—or any part of your book—and attract a sizeable number of blog readers or subscribers, you also assure publishers that a market of eager buyers exists for that book once it appears in print.

The majority of blog-to-book deals come to authors whom simply blog and garner a large number of unique readers and subscribers. It's less common for bloggers to blog a book. However, for aspiring authors, blogging a book makes great sense. You kill several birds with one stone: You write your book quickly in post-sized bits (300 to 500 word pieces), you build author platform, you self-publish your work, and you promote your work. For writers who don't like to build platform or promote their work, blogging a book offers a superb solution. They can do what they are good at—write—and what they need to do as well—build platform and promote their work. And they can get their books written.

How to Blog a Book

Here are some tips on how to begin blogging a book:

1. **Choose a topic.** Choose a topic that interests you and that interests a lot of people. Also pick a topic you feel passionate about since you'll be covering it for a long time—long past the conclusion of the book.

2. **Map out your book's content.** Do a mind map of the content for you blogged book. Start with your topic, and create lots of subtopics and sub-subtopics. Group these into chapters.

3. **Break your content into post-sized pieces.** Blog posts tend to range from 300 to 500 words, though some can run longer. Take the related subtopics and sub-subtopics from #2 that you grouped into chapters, and break them down into post-sized pieces. Consider each subtopic and its related sub-subtopics as small bits of copy you will write. You will need many of these to flesh out your blogged book's content and create a full manuscript.

4. **Create a business plan for your book.** Make sure you identify markets online and off for your blogged book, that you analyze the competition so you are sure you've got a unique concept as a blogged book (or blog) and a printed book or e-book. Use this to plan your promotion, too. (Find more information on how to do this in *The Author Training Manual: Develop Marketable Ideas, Craft Books That Sell, Become the Author Publishers Want, and Self-Publish Effectively*.)

5. **Set up a blog.** You need a blog. If you don't know how to create one yourself, hire a webmaster or a blog specialist. The free blogs, like those hosted by WordPress, are pretty easy to set up if you're a beginner. I recommend you get a self-hosted blog, though.

6. **Start writing your blogged book.** Compose your posts using a word processing program so you create a manuscript. Just write 300 to 500 words per day or several times a week. Post this to your blog each of the days you write. Even if you only write an average of 350 words per day three times a week, you'll have 1,050 per week. That's 4,200 per month. In 12 months, you'll have written 50,400 words—the first draft of your manuscript. Write and publish more posts per week, and your book will get it written faster.

When you're done, start editing, revising, adding content, etc. Create new material as well, so your book has additional copy that can't be found on your blog.

To blog a book in a month, you might create a series of 30 related posts and write and publish them over the course of the month. Produce them first in a word-processing program, and then copy and paste into your blog. By the end of the month you'll have a manuscript for a short book.

How to Book a Blog

Here are a few tips you can use if you've been blogging consistently and would like to repurpose your blog content into a printed book or e-book, which my colleague Joel Friedlander, a book designer and author, calls "booking a blog":

1. **Identify a topic for your book.** Your blog may be finely honed to one topic making it easy to choose a topic, or you may have covered many diverse topics. Choose the one topic you think will make the best book. You may want to go through step #5

above to help you evaluate your book idea's success potential prior to beginning the project. Or look at your blog analytics to see which posts received the most page views over time to help you decide what your readers might be most interested in reading off line.

2. **Create a Table of Contents.** Create a structure for your book, and determine what content you need for that book. This content should not be determined by what is already on the blog but by how you can produce the best book possible. However, you may find most of what you need in your categories. When you blog, you catalog posts into categories. The titles of your categories may serve as chapter titles or simply repositories of major subject areas that should be chapters in your book. Look through your categories to identify subject areas to cover in your chapters. Then create a Table of Contents. Or do a mind map and use that to ideate the content for your book and to determine its structure.

3. **Create a document for your manuscript.** Create a document in a word processing program that you will use to create your manuscript. If you prefer, create one for each chapter. This will become your first draft of your book. Do whatever you want to prepare to begin dropping in blog posts you will be copying and pasting from your blogging program.

4. **Look through your categories to identify relevant blog posts.** Go back to your categories, and begin opening old blog posts relevant to the book. Copy and paste them into your word processing document.

5. **Search your blog content using tags to find more relevant blog posts.** Copy and paste these into your manuscript.

6. **Fill in the gaps in your content with new material.** Your existing blog posts may not cover all the material necessary for a "good" book. Be sure you create new content so you produce the best book possible while also providing your readers with something new they can't find on the blog.

When you're done, start editing, reorganizing, revising, adding content, etc.

Booking a blog represents a great way to write a book in a month. You don't have to write much new content. You spend most of your time compiling existing content and revising it.

Whether you blog a book or book a blog, you've used your talents as a writer to write, publish, and promote yourself using blog technology.

Write the Draft of a Short Memoir in One Month

By Denis Ledoux

While memoirs are often lengthy and encompass an entire lifetime and so take years to write, it is also possible to produce a draft of a short memoir in one month.

By definition, an autobiography is a story of one's entire life, and a memoir is the story of a certain time of your life, or of a topic (theme) of one's life: e.g., starting and growing my business, taking care of my aging parents, coming to terms with my divorce, etc. A memoir can also consist of snippets of life. So . . .

Keep in mind that I am thinking of a short memoir here, not a comprehensive autobiography.

What Ought a Short Memoir Be About?

Start the month by selecting a memoir topic that is important to you. That may seem a no-brainer, but I have witnessed many people write not about their important material but about the material they deem easy to write about or "more interesting." Inevitably, because they do not access the energy of their inner self that is yearning to be heard, they slip into "the writer's block," into a failure of energy.

You will write well and voluminously if you are motivated by your interest in the subject matter. Choose a topic that you are viscerally interested to share.

A Key Tool: "The Core Memory List"

1. **A core memory list contains only those items or highlights that are most important to you in the period (or about the topic) that is your subject.** These are the events, relationships, settings, people, and feelings without which, in the context of your subject, you would not today be who you are.

   For instance, for me, the core list of a memoir of my high school years was limited to:

   - My relationship with my teachers.

   - Friendships.

   - My evolving attachment to some of my studies.

   - The role of religion in my life.

   At this point in the process, I was still in the pre-writing stage—as you should be. I was getting the material for my stories organized so that, when I sit down to write, the writing will come easily. In addition, I will be helped by having selected the most important of my high-school experiences to write about.

   The point at this early stage of lifewriting is to begin the process of understanding what happened in your life. As you try to understand, and eventually to write, the broader picture, you will find this work of paring down the memories of a time/topic into its core memory list to be very valuable in creating a focus.

2. **A core memory list helps you to start writing.** It will be especially important to you as you commit to writing a memoir draft in a month because, when you sit to write and find yourself staring at a blank page or screen, your core memory list will suggest to you what to write about. No more writer's block!

3. **Under each of your core memories, create a sub-core list.** In my high school list, I wrote memories about the most important of my teachers (those who were most formative for me). Here I made notes of their teaching philosophy, their style, etc. I looked for similarities between the different teachers to see if I can understand something about my own needs at that time.

   I also wrote about the various subjects: about why they interested me or not, about the influence of the subject on me, etc.

4. **A core memory list assures that you are undertaking your most important stories first.** If, for whatever reason, you do not finish writing all your stories, you will not be left with a number of insignificant ones instead of the pivotal ones you had intended to record. Once you have preserved the highlight experiences of your short memoir, then you can turn to writing others as you have the time. (I have had several clients who died while writing long memoirs and so never finished them.)

5. **Not only will your core memory list suggest the parameters of your topic and thus create economy in writing, but the sub-lists will also help you to fill out each of your core stories.** When you cluster memories under core headings, you easily know such details as who was there, what the place looked like, what was going on in your life before and after the memory list item, etc.

6. Essentially, because you've done extensive pre-writing in the first days of your month-long memoir project, you will find that the actual writing is a breeze.

7. Remember: "Yard by yard, it's hard. Inch by inch, it's a cinch!"

Building Your Core Memory List

- In order to compile your core memory list, select no more than ten items. Ten is large enough to make this list somewhat comprehensive. It is also small enough to force you to make decisions about the importance of each item. (You ought not to have more than ten core items, but you may have fewer.)

- Place your core memory list in your three-ring memoir-writing binder. This makes the task of reviewing your list easy.

Thirty Days to a Short Memoir

By Denis Ledoux

It's possible to get your first draft of a memoir done in a month's time. To do so during National Nonfiction Writing Month (NaNonFiWriMo) or at any time of the year, follow these simple instructions.

1. **Choose a period of your life to write about.** The strict definition of a memoir is the story of a certain time of your life, or of a topic (theme) of one's life, while an autobiography is the story of your entire life. (In practice or common usage, people use the terms interchangeably.) To meet the parameters of a month of writing, it would be easier for you to choose a period of your life rather than your entire life. You can write a memoir but perhaps not an autobiography.

2. **Set a decent amount of time aside to do the writing.** Schedule it. You HAVE to show up for the work. Wishing you were writing or feeling bad that you're not won't get your memoir written. The more time you set aside the more you will write and the more likely you will be to meet your goal of writing a memoir in a month.

3. **Let go of having to write deathless prose on your first draft.** What you are accomplishing this month is getting the flow of your story down in a first draft. Your rewriting will have to take place later in your second write through. (This polishing stage will occur in another month.)

4. **Gather your support material prior to the start of the month.** That includes photographs, journals, clippings, and photocopies. Read them and become familiar with their contents.

5. **Follow the day-to-day suggestions listed below.** If you are starting late, do November 1 today—whatever the date (or month) is—and proceed for the next 30 days. It's also permissible to do "one" day in two or three or more days. Think of these as steps or units of activity. You will find it useful to read through the list and, if you feel the need to reorder the list, do so to meet your need. This is about you. Depending on the time you can allot daily, you may be able to write more than the recommended assignment. In that case, go back to a previous day, and follow it once more.

November 1: Create a Memory List of your life consisting of at least 200 items. (See page 41 of my _Turning Memories into Memoirs: A Handbook for Writing Lifestories._) At this point, this list is derived solely from memory.

November 2: Remember as many details of an event from early on in the memoir story line as you can. Take notes on what you recall.

November 3: Write a story or a vignette from an item on your Memory List. Remember that this is a first draft.

November 4: Find your memorabilia (diplomas, newspaper articles, certificates, letter) from your memoir timeframe, and Memory List at least 50 memories that come to you. Write as many vignettes as you can in the time left that you have allotted to write.

November 5: Share one of your lifestories (from November 3 and 4) with someone who was not part of the stories. Ask them for reactions. What more would they have liked to know? What didn't "ring true" for them? What questions remained unanswered? Rework the vignette as soon as possible after this session to address these issues.

November 6: Organize a lifestory party at which you invite your friends, your siblings, and/or other people who might be able contribute to your info gathering. This is not a social gathering but an information-harvesting event. Tell your guests there will be a free exchange of memories that you will record because you are writing a memoir

November 7: Relate a vignette from your memoir timeframe to your child/grandchild, friend, and/or relative. Record it as you speak. Your object is to experience how it feels to tell a story to a person. Does telling feel different from writing? Again, ask yourself and them the following: What more would you/they have liked to know? What didn't "ring true" for you/them? What questions remained unanswered? Write the spoken vignette as soon as possible after this session.

November 8: Narrate to someone the backstory of an experience that occurred during the timeframe of your memoir. This is an experience that needs a flashback in the memoir as an explanation. Ask yourself and your listener(s) the following. What more would you/they have liked to know? What didn't "ring true" for you/them? What questions remained unanswered? Write the vignette as soon as possible after this session.

November 9: Write a journal entry about a day in your memoir time frame. Include salient details that will make the day as vivid as it was right after you lived it. Use this entry to write a story. The difference between a journal entry and a memoir story is that a memoir vignette has to be structured with a plot line. Journals are more free-flowing. Write the vignette as soon as possible after the journal entry.

November 10: Write a 3-to-5-page story about an incident in your memoir timeframe that was pivotal in getting you to resolve the problem you were facing. Remember that John loves Mary and Mary loves John is not a story plot or problem to be resolved. John loves Mary and Mary loves John and John also loves Peter, however, has the making of a story plot. Structure your stories around problems.

November 11: Write three to five pages of another person's role in your lifestory. Use the five senses to include salient details.

November 12: Reading day. Select a memoir from a bookstore or library that covers some of the same topic as the memoir you are writing. For instance, if you are writing about healing from an illness, select a memoir about healing. Begin reading and keep reading everyday until you are finished.

November 13: View a movie that is a biography. Observe how the camera interprets the story. How can you use the sensibility of the camera to include more details in your stories? How do you need to write to give the reader the sense of "seeing" the story? If you can, rework a story as soon as possible after viewing the film.

November 14: Travel to a place that figures in your memoir. Photograph it for later referral or for including in the book. Memory List the old memories and the new that arise. Write as much as you can in the time remaining to you today.

November 15: Read history (a book, an article, a web posting) of your region, your ethnic group, your industry, your religion, or your city to better understand the period of your life you are writing about. Note details you can incorporate into your story. Sit down and write a vignette that either incorporates new data or is inspired by the use of particular data that you are drawing from your Memory List.

November 16: Go to a museum that features a topic that is prominent in understanding your time frame. (For example, if your story is about serving in the military, visit a military museum.) Note details you can incorporate into your story. Write or rewrite a story as soon as possible—preferably that day.

November 17: Today sit down with your Memory List, and write as long as you can on as many items on it as possible.

November 18: Visualize yourself at a certain time in your memoir. In your mind, scrutinize the scene that comes to mind. Who is there?

What are they doing? What details are clear to you? Incorporate as much as you can into your lifestory writing today.

November 19: Print out on white paper the stories you have written, and place them in a three-ring binder. Reread your vignettes. Are there linking stories missing? Take a colored sheet of paper and write the topic of the missing story (or stories) on it. Write development notes on this colored paper. Write a missing story.

November 20: Read a story you have written. Go through it with a magic marker. Highlight all general descriptions. Nice plan, great day, wonderful dress, etc. Now replace general descriptions with specific words: effective, step-by-step plan; a day filled with play and rest and much intimate conversation; a peau-de-soie dress with a knee-length hem. Using specific words, write a story inspired from your Memory List.

November 21: Ask someone to read an excerpt of your memoir out loud. You are now the audience. How complete and satisfying does the story sound to you? Take notes on what you feel may be missing. Request the reader to ask you questions about the reading excerpt. Rewrite your story if necessary to make it clearer. Do so as soon as possible. This can be a learning exercise in being sensitive to the qualities of what makes an effective editor.

November 22: If you don't have enough photos for your memoir, explore web-based photo repositories for appropriate photos. Write new stories stimulated by those photographs.

November 23: Sit down with your Memory List and write as long as you can on as many items on it as possible. Alternately, write a story noted on a colored paper in your three-ring binder.

November 24: A memoir depicts a hero's journey. There is a problem that you have resolved (or not), and that trajectory provides the core of your memoir. The crisis of the memoir is when you are about to crumble under the stress and tension of the problem. The problem then usually has a moment when the main character (you) was able to step into the future. This is the turning point. Write or rewrite a story about the crisis and the turning point. Repeat this exercise for as many stories as is feasible. (Some stories are merely transition stories and do not call for problem solving.)

November 25: Reread stories that take place early in your memoir's timeline. Introduce phrases and sentences that generate foreshadowing and suspense. "Little did I know then that . . ." "What if I could not sustain this level of attention . . . ?" This is an effective tool in creating interest. (This is also a dangerous tool that risks slipping into cliché fast.)

November 26: Write the first (introductory, initial) pages of your memoir. These pages should pose a problem, be set at a time when you were completely involved in the problem, and begin at some point close to the ending. For example, if this were a memoir about a divorce, you cannot reasonably start at your first date. (That would be too taxing on the reader!) Instead, you would do better to start in a marriage counseling session when it becomes evident to you that this marriage will have to come to an end. Subsequently, you can utilize flashbacks to provide both information and feeling.

November 27: You have been writing intuitively—creating stories as the unconscious and my notes prompt you. Today, let's go cerebral: write a timeline. Organize your timeline according to values: some events and actions are pivotal; others are supportive and flow from other decisions. The pivotal events and actions are your chapter headings while the supportive material is part of the chapter. Write stories that are still missing.

November 28: Go through your stories and introduce direct dialog. "He said he would not come" is indirect dialog. It can be changed to direct dialog "He said, 'I will come'." Many adjectives can be changed into dialog. "She was angry" can become "Don't you ever speak to me in that tone again, or I'll knock you down. I don't care where we are!"

November 29: Go through your stories and change descriptions into actions. "She was angry" can become "She picked a plate up from the dish rack and flung it across the room. The plate crashed against the door, inches from my head. Rework as many stories as you can.

November 30: Set up a schedule to either finish the first draft or begin the second (polishing up) draft. In the time remaining, keep writing.

Six Easy Steps to Writing a Profitable E-Book in 30 Days

By Ellen Violette

To write a profitable e-book in 30 days you first have to properly plan to write an e-book in 30 days. And the way you do that is to lay out what you would have to complete each day and then pencil in your plan working backward from day 30 to day 1.

Creating a plan can be broken down into the following 6 steps:

Step 1. Doing the research

Before you can write a profitable e-book, you MUST do the research first. This will tell you what your market wants to buy as well as what keywords and phrases will get them to take action. It's then your job to figure out what you can offer and deliver it in the way that will excite them and get them to purchase it from you.

Step 2. Organizing your e-book

Consider the organization of your e-book before you write. Do you need sections and chapters or just chapters? If you need sections, will they be chronological? Or by subject? Or organized in some other way?

Step 3. Creating your call to action

Your call-to-action can often influence the direction your e-book will take, so you always want to figure out what it is BEFORE you write your e-book.

The call to action is what you want readers to do after they finish reading the book, such as purchase another book or a program or service. Keep the offer you make in your e-book for your next product—the actual call to action—at $97 or less, unless you send people to a teleseminar, webinar, or video presentation first.

Step 4. Writing time

If you create six chapters, you have eight points in each chapter, and you write two pages per point, each chapter would be 16 pages. This would give you an e-book of 96 pages. Since you need time to complete the other pieces for your e-book, you need to write your e-book in about a two-week period, which would mean you'd have to write six pages a day during that time. If you want a larger e-book, you'll have to write more; for a smaller e-book, you'll write less.

Step 5. Finishing time

Authors often forget that there is more to writing an e-book or book than the actual chapters. You'll need to add additional pages, such as the table of contents, about the author page, limit of liability, etc., to complete your project.

Step 6. Title and chapter heading writing

Titles and chapter headings need to catch the reader's attention, and that can take time. If you're going to write them yourself, you'll need to leave enough time to get them right. Otherwise consider outsourcing them. That's what I did when I wrote Sell More E-Books: Low & No-Cost Tactics to EXPLODE Your E-Book Sales and Downloads (www.sellmoreeBooks.com) with Jim Edwards on a 30-day schedule.

If you're on a budget, you might want to look into using vendors on Fiverr at: www.fiverr.com. It's a very inexpensive way to get the help you need creating title and chapter headings. Be sure to find vendors who are at least Level 1 vendors. Level 2 and Top Sellers are even better.

With the right planning, anyone can write a profitable e-book (or book) in 30 days or less. Follow these six steps, and in just 30 days or less, you too can be ready to publish your e-book or book!

How to Write a Lead-Generating Kindle Book

By Kristen Eckstein

The hot method to generating online leads used to be to write a free report, link it to an email opt-in form on your website, and deliver it to your target audience in exchange for their email. Now that email newsletters and marketing have saturated the market, and people are tired of spending hours of their time sifting through email, this method rarely works to generate highly qualified leads anymore. Now people are looking for action steps, checklists, video tutorials, and other resources to give them instant results, which are great free offers for your website.

So what should you do with all those free reports gathering virtual dust on your hard drive? Is the report-delivery method completely dead?

Enter Amazon Kindle Direct Publishing (KDP). Now, with Amazon KDP, you can turn those reports into targeted, qualified leads and residual cash flow. Why Kindle? The top-selling electronic device in all of 2012 on Amazon.com was the Kindle Fire HD 7" tablet, and the second-best seller was the Kindle Paperwhite. The fourth best-selling device was the Kindle 6" E Ink Display. Sixty-seven percent of e-books sold are purchased through the Kindle Store, followed by 25 percent on BarnesandNoble.com and a mere 5 percent in iBooks. Needless to say, Kindle owns the e-reader market, so if you're not writing Kindle books you're missing out on some serious lead generation.

How should you structure your lead-generating Kindle book?

Length and Content

Kindle's minimum is 2,500 words, so think of short reports you already have that you can easily convert into a Kindle book. Your Kindle content does not have to be long if it delivers results.

Many readers get bored with books because they explain the same concept three or four different ways. This wordiness isn't necessary in how-to business-building Kindle books. Be straight, to the point, and share examples and stories of how your clients have followed your steps and seen results.

For example, my newest series of *Author's Quick Guide* Kindle books range at 4,000 words for the shortest one up to just over 12,000 words for the longest one. Start with a report you've already written or a blog post article with step-by-steps, and expand on each step with examples, stories, and images. (Hint: color pictures are great for Kindle books!) You'll be surprised how quickly you'll generate content by using something you've already written as the foundational outline.

An Engaging Opt-In

Like with a free report, the point of your Kindle book is to generate leads, right? To give your leads the chance to get more from you, and to get on your email list, create an opt-in that coincides with your Kindle book. For example, if your book is teaching step-by-steps or a system for how to market your business online, create a simple checklist of action steps and invite your readers to get your checklist for free from your website. Make your free gift valuable—something that will help your readers get fast results.

Place your invitation to get your free gift after the Introduction of your e-book and before the first chapter. Kindle algorithms work off your Table of Contents. Whatever the first entry in your TOC is (usually your Introduction or Foreword), that's where your book will first open on a Kindle reader. By placing your opt-in before the first chapter and after the first item in the TOC, your opt-in won't be missed. Embed a link in your call to action, such as "Click here to get this free checklist!" that links to the page on your website where readers can download your free gift.

For more opt-in ideas, check out my e-*book Author's Quick Guide to Making Money with Your 99-Cent Kindle Book.*

Affordable Pricing

If your Kindle book is short and will be used primarily for lead generation, price it at 99 cents. If your e-book contains more content and how-to steps, especially if it will deliver fast results to the reader's primary goal, price it between $2.99-3.49. Lead-generating Kindle books should not be priced higher, as those rates are reserved for more substantial how-to credibility-boosting books.

Use these steps to get your lead-generating Kindle book written today!

How to Write an eBook Fast and Publish It in 30 Days or Less!

By Ellen Violette

The most time consuming part of writing an e-book is figuring out what you are going to write about (if you don't already know what niche you are going to be focusing on), determining how you are going to approach it so that it sounds fresh and worth reading, and deciding on the offer you are going to make in your eBook to get people to take the next step with you.

Find Your Niche and Perspective

You want a niche that is already selling, because then you know you'll have buyers. And you don't want a niche where you have to educate people to want what you have to offer, because that takes too long to get buyers. You want your potential buyers to already be on the edge of their seats with baited breath waiting for your e-book to go live!

That's why weight-loss e-books and books continue to be bestsellers. There's a new diet every week, and what works for one person doesn't necessarily work for another. So, people who want to lose weight will buy several weight-loss e-books/books. If you look at weight-loss titles, you'll see that it's the unique approach of each one that makes it a bestseller, even though so many have come before it. For example:

Atkins Diet: Why Your Divorce From Bread and Pasta Will Increase Your Happiness Decrease Your Pant Size

The South Beach Diet: The Delicious, Doctor-Designed, Foolproof Plan for Fast and Healthy Weight Loss

The Zone: A Revolutionary Life Plan to Put Your Body in Total Balance for Permanent Weight Loss

Think and Grow Thin: The Revolutionary Diet and Weight-loss System That Will Change Your Life in 88 Days!

The Blood Sugar Solution: The UltraHealthy Program for Losing Weight, Preventing Disease, and Feeling Great Now!

The Dukan Diet: 2 Steps to Lose the Weight, 2 Steps to Keep It Off Forever

You get the picture.

The key in each one is to approach the subject from a new perspective.

Determine Your Offer

Once you've done that, figure out what your offer is going to be. Most authors don't make their money from e-book sales (although they can be lucrative) but by teaching people how to consume the information-with upsells that come after the eBook purchase.

Decide How to Publish

Next, decide how you are going to publish your e-book.

Are you going to publish on Kindle or use a self-publishing platform (your own website, your own affiliate program, or a 3rd party site) or both? I recommend that you do both, but what you do first depends on what you are trying to achieve (I'll say more about this later).

Write a Title

Next, you need to write a killer title, one that will capture the reader on an emotional level and gives the benefit of what they will discover by reading it.

Organize Your Book

Then, organize your eBook. Ask yourself, "What do I want to write about first?"

Then "What do I want to write about next?" etc., until you have six to eight chapter headings.

After looking at your chapter headings decide if you need sections in your e-book. These are groupings of chapters. It could be a chronology like *Help! This Move Is Driving Me Crazy! The Ultimate Guide to Organizing Your Move to Save Time, Money & Your Sanity* (formerly, *The Moving Cure*), which is in three sections: before the move, during the move, and after the move. Or it could be by subject, like a health e-book that might have an emotional, spiritual, and physical well-being section.

Then, decide what points you want to make in each chapter. Write them down.

Create a Writing Plan

And finally, once you've done the preliminary research, you MUST decide on a writing plan to get this done within 30 days.

Give yourself no more than two weeks to write your eBook, because you'll need the extra time to put the finishing touches on your e-book and get it ready for publishing.

Now you are ready to write your eBook.

Note: If you find yourself trying to edit or you're judging while you are writing it, try talking it instead. You can use a tape recorder, your phone's dictation or recording application, a voice to text service, or a 3rd party recording sit.

The Final Touches

Once you've finished writing, you have to add the other pieces that go into an eBook:

- Table of contents

- Inside cover page

- Author bio

- Copyright information

- Limit of liability (be sure to contact an attorney to do this properly)

- Your offer or upsell

- Resources (optional)

And then publish it.

Note: Publishing in Kindle is a lot faster and easier, but you generally don't make as much money as with DIY self-publishing (if you do it the right way). But, if you are trying to get it up and selling within a 30-day period, you'll probably want to start with Kindle.

Follow this step-by-step process, and in 30 days you'll be a published author!

FINISHING WHAT
YOU START

5 Tips to Help You Finish a 30-Day Writing Challenge

By Rachel Z. Cornell

You've made the commitment to complete a non-fiction writing project in 30 days. I'm excited for you and want to help ensure your success. Below are five tips my writing clients use all the time to make sure they finish what they start.

1. Don't Wait for the Mood to Hit You

Artist Chuck Close says, "Inspiration is for amateurs; the rest of us just show up and get to work." This means, you don't wait around to be in the mood to write or until you have a blissful five-hour block of time to sit down. You just show up, preferably at the same time every day. If you long for inspiration, consistency will help the muse know when to put you in her appointment book.

Regardless of how you feel, though, your job is to just show-up.

2. Write or Do Nothing

When you sit down to write, do one of two things: write or do nothing. If you choose nothing, sit on your hands. No surfing, talking on your phone, or even humming. Sit. It's perfectly okay to do nothing. Chances are, though, you will have a thought and will want to write it down. Then you're writing. If you commit to doing only one of these two things during your scheduled writing time, I promise you, you will make meaningful progress.

3. Get Rid of Distractions

To help you write or do nothing, rid yourself of some of the most common distractions, notably social media and the Internet. There are simple, inexpensive programs such as <u>Freedom</u>, that are designed to lock you out of the internet or tempting websites for a set amount of time. Install one of these programs.

If, like me, your best writing time is the morning, then set your internet lockout software up before you go to bed. Lock yourself out so you're not allowed online until you complete your scheduled morning writing time. This will save you from one of the most prose-killing monsters of modern life: your inbox. Most of these programs allow for specified sites to stay active. This is good if you want to use the following online tool.

4. Use the Power of Accountability

Pair a short, well-defined and quantifiable action with positive peer pressure, and you're practically unstoppable. That's what Patti, a two-time documentary writer/producer discovered. Patti told me, "I finished both my documentaries one sentence at a time on your chat." People from all over the world stop by to work on and finish their projects one small action at a time.

Here's how the chat works. You identify a specific task you want to take. Maybe you want to write the first paragraph for a chapter. You "open a bookend" by typing your action into the chat box. As soon as you submit the action, you go do the work. When you're finished, "close the bookend" by returning to the chat and saying you're done. There's usually a person or two in the room, and people are always eager to cheer each other on.

5. Untangle Your Tongue

If you're like every other person who writes, there are times when little details or too many voices in your head get in the way of your good ideas. You can cut through all the noise in a heart beat. At the start of each sentence just write, "What I mean to say is . . ." I really hope you try this because it's remarkably effective. Once you finish your writing session, go back, delete all your "what I mean to says," and tah-dah! You're a super genius.

Super genius and committed author, that is. Writing isn't easy. Distractions, isolation, lack of clarity, and doubt thwart your efforts, but now you have a few sexy tools and tips that will keep you moving.

How to Keep the Energy Going

By Nina Amir

As with any deadline, when National Nonfiction Writing Month, or any write-a-book-in-a-month challenge, ends, so does the increased energy and focus that helped you rise to meet that challenge. Such a challenge is meant to prove that you can, indeed, work quickly and get a lot done in a short amount of time if you set your mind to it. Now, you'll have to find ways to generate your own motivation and willpower to start and finish nonfiction projects without the deadline of a formal challenge or contest or the energy that comes from knowing others are completing projects along with you.

The lack of an outside deadline or accountability can pose the largest hurdle for a writer. That's why I'd like to focus upon how to "stick to it"—meaning your writing.

How do you actually stick to the whole process from start to finish and get your writing out into the world so it can be read? How do you now, after a month of hard work, take the first draft of your manuscript and revise it, then get it to a professional editor (and work with the editor on more revisions), write a query letter, send letters to agents, write a proposal, or self-publish your book? How do you do these things rather than just deciding you are tired and would rather read a novel or watch your favorite television show?

Getting published takes great will, courage, passion, determination, persistence, and drive—things we don't always possess. You can do some things to help yourself develop these characteristics and follow through on the things necessary to get your writing out in to the world. Here are 10 tips to help you stick to it and continue moving forward until next year when the Write Nonfiction in November Challenge begins again or the next time you want to write a book in a month.

1. **Find an accountability partner.** Find someone—another writer is best, but it can be anyone (preferably not a spouse or romantic partner)—to whom you can make an accounting each week, every two weeks or once a month. This is a person to whom you will make commitments, such as: "I will write and finish my query letter this week"; "I will have my proposal done by our next phone call"; "I will have sent out five proposals by our next meeting"; or "I will write five pages every day this month." You can also offer them dates: "I will post six blogs by December 10th." If you have a writing group, you can use the members of this group as your accountability partners.

2. **Get a freelance editor or book coach.** When you are paying an editor, you are more likely to work hard at your writing and to try and finish your project in a timely manner. Plus, your editor may give you deadlines. Additionally, working with someone on your book or project keeps you motivated and focused. Often people hire a book coach to help them do just that and to give them monthly deadlines and make them accountable for a certain amount of work each month. If you really can't stick to it alone, a <u>book coach</u> can help you do so all the way until the very end—a published project.

3. **Make writing and submitting work your #1 priority.** Yes, we all need to build platform, promote our books and ourselves, make money, handle life's demands, and answer email, but commit to making these things lower on your priority list. Make writing and submitting your work priority #1 by simply taking this task on first every day. Yes, first. Don't look in your email box first. Don't make phone calls first. Don't see who wrote on your FaceBook "wall" and find a few more "friends." Write first. Submit your writing first. Otherwise, if you make

these tasks even priority #3 or #4, many days you won't get around to accomplishing them.

4. **Use a reward system.** This works for adults as well as for children. If need be, bribe yourself with a reward for getting your writing and submitting done. Maybe your reward is a walk with a friend or a trip to Starbucks. Maybe it's 30 minutes on FaceBook or reading a book. Maybe it's a pile of Hershey's Kisses. It matters not what reward you receive as long as it's something you appreciate and that will motivate you to do what you need to do to stick to your nonfiction writing and to the getting-published process.

5. **Use timed writings.** If you feel like you just don't normally have a lot of time to devote to any aspect of your nonfiction writing, take on the tasks in short bursts. Work for 15 minutes on any aspect of your project. Set a timer for whatever amount of time you have, and then write as fast as you can until the timer goes off. Don't edit as you write.

6. **Blog your book.** Many an author has been discovered via his or her blog. Plus, it's a great way to write a book in short increments. Plus, blogging seems less intimidating than sitting down to write a whole book. Simply commit to writing three or four paragraphs of a post—or one screen's worth of copy— each day on the subject of your book, and see where it goes. Have an outline of your book in front of you, and stick to it as much as possible, but allow yourself to go with the flow of blogging. You'll find writing much easier, and you'll be publishing as you go! (Blogging also can serve as a great way to move through writer's block; write fast and as if you are talking to a friend. That moves you through your block.)

7. **Keep your goal in mind.** Remember why you chose to write this particular project and what you want to get out of writing, completing and publishing it. Who will it serve? How will it help? Why is it important to say what you have to say?

Or simply remember the fact that your goal is to become a published author. You can't accomplish that goal if you don't continually write and submit your work—and overcome the fear of your work being rejected by simply submitting yet again. You might want to create a "vision board" to remind yourself of this goal. A vision board consists of a poster board (or something smaller if you prefer) covered in pictures and sayings that represent your goal. It's a visual reminder of what you desire to accomplish. Hang it in your office so you can see it whenever you look up from your computer.

8. **Acknowledge and remember the greater purpose to your writing.** Some writers feel the reason they write comes from a deep place within them . . . from their soul. It's their soul's purpose to write. If you feel this way, each time you sit down to "work," remind yourself that you are not simply working; you are fulfilling your purpose here in the world. This may ring especially true for you if you are writing books in the self-help, inspirational, or human potential categories.

9. **Move through your fear.** Why do most writers not stick to their writing or to the submission process? They are afraid . . . afraid of failure, afraid of rejection, afraid of being seen, afraid of speaking their truth, afraid their families will disapprove of what they've written, afraid of being out in front of lots of people, even afraid of success. You must move through your fear. Fear never helped anyone become successful. It only stopped them from achieving that which they most desired. Each time you feel afraid, sit down at your computer and write or put together a submission packet. Susan Jeffers' book title says it best, "Feel the Fear and Do It Anyway."

10. **Plan your work, and work you plan.** My son received this bit of advice in a fortune cookie at a Chinese restaurant. It was the perfect final tip to offer. Come up with a daily and weekly plan for your writing and for submitting what you write, and then work that plan. Don't deviate from your plan (unless it isn't

working). Decide when you will write and for how long. Then, do it. Give yourselves deadlines, and stick to them. Choose publications, editors, agents, and publishing houses that look promising, and then make a plan for when you will submit to them. Then, mail those submissions by those dates. Be your own worst boss . . . the one you are afraid of telling that you missed the deadline. And re-evaluate your work and your plan regularly—each day, each week, each month. Plan your work, and work your plan.

I've heard best-selling author Wayne Dyer say, "Don't die with your song still in you." In this case, I'll turn the statement around and say, "Don't die—or show up next year—with your nonfiction book still in you." Get it out! Try several of these tips, and commit to using at least one or two. In this way you will not only put the finishing touches on your book but get it published after your 30-day challenge ends.

How to Overcome the Only Obstacle Between You and Writing a Book in a Month

By Nina Amir

Our society perpetuates the belief that you must overcome numerous obstacles to succeed. These might include high levels of skill or knowledge, large amounts of time, vast quantities of money, and connections with the right people. While some of this may be true, only one real obstacle blocks the way to your success in any life arena–including writing a book in a month and later publishing it. If you remove it, the other hurdles become easy to overcome.

Can you identify the obstacle?

You.

You are in your own way. Specifically, your habitual behaviors and mindsets create internal hurdles you must constantly try to jump or remove. These include how you react to situations, your thoughts about circumstances and people, and your beliefs about writing a book in 30 days. When you conquer—or change—your habitual habits and mindsets you allow yourself to reach your writing and publishing goals and create your dream career as a writer and author.

Personal Growth Makes Writing Easier

Suppose you ask authors how they became successful. They likely will say they worked hard, acquired skills and knowledge, and were diligent, committed, and tenacious in pursuing their writing goals. Most also will tell you they "worked on themselves." In other words, they engaged in some sort of personal growth or development.

High performers know their own behavioral and mental tendencies either slow down or speed up their ability to achieve success. Only if they take time for personal change can they alter those tendencies and succeed professionally or personally.

And so, they invest in themselves by joining masterminds, programs, and courses. They hire therapists and coaches. And they read books about self-improvement and apply what they learn.

These efforts help them change their identity, behavior, and mindset. As a result, achieving success in any life arena becomes much easier.

What Happens When You Get Out of the Way

Here's are two examples demonstrating how getting out of your own way (changing yourself) enhances your ability to succeed.

I had a client who believed he couldn't complete his writing projects. He would describe himself as "someone who never finishes what he starts." That was his identity.

As a result, he found it tough to succeed at anything, including becoming an author. That makes sense since you do need to complete manuscripts (or other writing projects) to become an author.

This man rarely started anything new, including pursuing writing ideas, for fear he would disappoint himself again. His mind was focused on thoughts like, "Why start? I won't finish," or "If I start and don't finish, I'll just feel horrible about myself, so I won't bother." Thus, he looked at his life through that lens (mindset) and only saw incomplete projects.

His behavior followed suit. He didn't start new projects—no matter how important they were to him. He maintained a noteBook filled

168

with book ideas, but he never acted on them. And if he did start, he inevitably didn't finish.

Then he decided to invest in personal development and became one of my coaching clients. He identified a few past short book projects he had finished, which helped him realize he could and had completed things previously. This insight helped him change his belief about himself and, therefore his identity. He used the knowledge that he was someone who completes projects to help him finish his current projects and then future ones, too.

Also, he decided to stop disappointing himself. Instead, he chose to be self-integral and keep his promises to himself. With two new ways of seeing himself—as someone who completes projects and someone who has self-integrity, not only did his mindset shift, but his behaviors, too.

He began thinking, "I finish what I start" and "If I say I will finish something, I do because I have self-integrity." Eventually, these became his beliefs and, therefore, his mindset. He proved that this was true each time he completed a book project or achieved a writing or publishing goal.

So, he began taking on writing projects and required himself to finish on a deadline. His new habit was to finish something before starting a new project or goal. As a result, he began consistently finishing the writing projects he started.

As you can imagine, the changes this man made in his identity, mindset and habits made all the difference in his ability to succeed as a writer and author.

Another one of my clients self-published a book on parenting, but she didn't know how—and didn't think she could—monetize her expertise and book with courses or programs. She told me, "I'm not a good businessperson. Plus, I'm horrible with technology." These were her identities, and her habits and mindsets aligned with them perfectly.

She did not approach authorship as a businessperson, and, therefore, rarely promoted her books. Nor did she see authorship from a business perspective; in her mind, she was an artist. And she refused to create an author website, use social media as a promotional tool, or explore ways to coach clients, create courses, or share her knowledge via any type of audio or video tool. She insisted that all these tasks were simply "too techie" for her to try.

Yet, she wanted to support herself. After a few coaching sessions, she admitted that she hadn't known how to write or publish a book, but she figured it out and did so successfully. Therefore, she was someone with the ability to figure things out. That identity would serve her well as she explored the business side of her chosen career and the technology that would allow her to monetize her book. As a result of adopting this identity, she enrolled in a program that would teach her how to create and promote courses.

She also chose to be someone willing to tackle new and difficult tasks. "I'll honor the challenge," she told me. And this new identity allowed her to learn how to use social media and do all the things she learned in the online-course building program in which she invested.

Her mindset and habits aligned with her two new identities—"I am someone with the ability to figure things out" and "I am someone who honors a challenge," which made it much easier for her to do what was necessary to become an <u>authorpreneur</u>. In fact, less than a year later, she launched a membership program for parents that featured prerecorded video lessons coupled with live virtual coaching sessions. She also marketed it on social media and now earns enough per month to pay her mortgage.

That's the power of doing personal growth work. You stop being the obstacle to your success and, instead, become a person who can do the things necessary to create the success you desire.

Your Habitual Behaviors

Unhelpful habitual behaviors take many forms. For example, you might react with anger whenever someone cuts you off in traffic, hit the snooze button daily when the morning alarm rings, or spend too much time scrolling on social media (rather than writing). Or, like my client, you might habitually start writing projects you don't finish or say you can't do something because you aren't "that type of person." These habits don't help you succeed.

Not only that, they are reactions rather than responses. Reactions are habitual or unconscious ways of behaving in certain situations. Often, something triggers you—like the jerk who cut you off or the sound of the morning alarm—and you react in the same way as always.

On the other hand, responses are intentional and conscious. For example, you decide how to behave when someone cuts you off, like taking a deep breath and feeling grateful that you didn't get in an accident. Or you choose to get out of bed when the alarm rings so you have time to work on your book before you have to go to work or get the kids off to school.

Reactions reap negative results. They don't help you progress toward success—and sometimes even cause you to move backward a few steps. Responses have a higher probability of positive results because you choose them intentionally as a way to achieve a goal. Therefore, they successfully help you get from Point A to Point B, like from unpublished to published or from the start of a book project to finished in 30 days.

Your Habitual Mindsets

Unhelpful habitual mindsets are created by unsupportive thoughts you think repeatedly. If you think a thought often enough, it becomes a belief. And all your beliefs influence your mindset.

Many of your repetitive thoughts stem from early programming or life experiences. For instance, someone influential—like a parent, teacher, or coach—told you something, and you chose to believe it. They "programmed" you to think you were intelligent, stupid, talented, untalented, good at business, bad at business, for instance.

Or you had an experience, like being rejected by a literary agent. You choose to interpret that event to mean something specific. Maybe you decided you are someone who doesn't have salable ideas, isn't a good enough writer, or doesn't have the credentials to get traditionally published.

Such thoughts become your beliefs and then your mindset. And your mindset becomes the lens through which you see the world, including your experiences and the people you meet . . . and yourself.

Let's say you have published 50 or more articles in magazines. Yet, most of your life, you believed you weren't a good writer. When you look at your clip file, you see the articles but think, "I'm not a good enough writer. After all, I haven't published a book, and good writers are authors." Your mindset clouds your vision and doesn't allow you to acknowledge that you are a good and accomplished writer. Thus, you'll never feel confident about your writing.

However, if you believe you are a good writer—and are grateful for the publications that featured your work—you see yourself and your circumstances differently. Your mindset provides a lens that helps you see your worth and value as a writer. And that mindset helps you act in ways that make you successful...including achieving your goal of becoming an author.

Or let's say life experiences have caused you to believe you aren't good enough. You see everything through this lens. You won't think you are good enough to attract a literary agent or book publishing deal. In fact, you'll never feel good enough for anything in the writing and publishing world or in any other life arena.

A not-good-enough mindset is an obstacle to success. It keeps you stuck wondering if you are good enough to tackle any challenge successfully—including writing a book in a month.

Change your mindset, though, and your ability to complete a book-in-a-month challenge and achieve successful authorship changes. When you are good enough, you have the confidence to take on a 30-day writing challenge, query an agent and send a book proposal to a publisher. And you have the confidence to do whatever it takes to become an author. In fact, you'll know you are good enough to pursue your craziest writing and publishing dream. You'll see yourself differently, and your results will be different.

The same holds true when you change any thoughts or beliefs related to becoming an author. Rid yourself of all the negative mental chatter, like "I can't do it," "I'm not techie," "I'm too old," or "I am overwhelmed." Replace those thoughts and beliefs with positive ones, and you will form more positive and supportive habits. You'll also see yourself and the world from a totally different perspective—one that helps you become an author.

How to Remove the One Obstacle to Success

Removing the obstacle—you—involves changing your habitual behaviors and mindsets. You accomplish this by becoming intentional and aware of your actions and thoughts. Habits tend to be unconscious. Thus, you must bring them into your consciousness.

Do this by identifying two life arenas first:

- an area in which you feel successful.

- an area in which you feel challenged.

Next, write down the thoughts and behaviors you have related to each.

For example, maybe you feel challenged in the life arena of business and authorpreneurship. Thus, you might think you don't have the skills or knowledge to monetize your book with products and services. As a result, you no longer submit work to publications or to agents or publishers. Or you've stopped writing at all.

Perhaps you feel successful as a parent. You might think, "I'm a good parent," or "Parenting comes naturally to me." As a result, you do whatever it takes to care for your children without hesitation. You make decisions about their well-being and find solutions to parenting problems without doubt regarding your ability to "get it right."

Notice that, in the areas where you succeed, you have positive thoughts and well-planned or confident responses. In the areas you feel challenged, you have negative thoughts, unplanned reactions, or lack of confidence.

Once you have gone through this exercise, your next step involves applying your "success strategies" to the areas where you find it harder to succeed. These are the behaviors and mindsets that help you succeed. For instance, your confidence as a parent could be applied to your writing challenges.

Or you can write new positive thoughts or affirmations to repeat consciously to yourself. Also, decide how to act or respond, choosing ways you feel will result in success.

Three Essentials Necessary for Getting Out of Your Way

Getting out of your own way isn't really that hard. It takes three essential things:

1. *The willingness to take responsibility for your current behaviors and mindsets.* Once you have done that, you can also be responsible for changing the ones that don't serve you.

2. *Awareness of your behaviors and mindsets.* When you know what you are thinking and doing that makes you an obstacle, you can change them. This moves you out of the way.

3. *The determination to succeed.* As with any endeavor, determination is essential. To successfully remove the obstacle blocking your success, you must be committed to making personal changes that help you succeed.

There is no reason to overcome many hurdles on your way to success as a writer and author. Instead, overcome the one obstacle blocking your path—you. Decide who you need to be to accomplish your writing goals, including writing a book in a month. Then, your mindsets and habits align with your new identity and the hurdles disappear or become easy to overcome.

CONCLUSION

Author Attitude Ensures You Finish What You Start.

By Nina Amir

Much of finishing anything you start—a book-in-a-month challenge, an exercise program, a diet, or an online course—has to do with your attitude. Without the right attitude, you're almost doomed to fail from the beginning.

I believe every author needs to possess four essential elements to succeed. However, you can also apply them specifically to writing a book in a month. For this reason, I'd like to share with you an excerpt from *The Author Training Manual: A Comprehensive Guide to Writing Books that Sell*, which I've adapted for use here. It explains these four elements.

The Four Elements of Author Attitude

The most successful people in the world will tell you that, more than anything else, their attitude helped them achieve their goals. If you want to succeed as an author, you need more than a good idea and writing skill. You need an Author Attitude.

Author Attitude consists of four primary characteristics:

1. Willingness
2. Optimism
3. Objectivity

4. Tenacity

I have arranged the four characteristics of Author Attitude to create an acronym to help you remember them. It spells a word that you'll be saying when it helps you finish your 30-day challenge: WOOT!

Let's look at each characteristic.

Willingness. To become a successful author you need a general willingness to change and grow. Your old attitudes, actions, behaviors, thoughts, decisions, beliefs, and habits have only gotten you this far. They helped you achieve your current results. If you want a new level of success as a writer, something has to change. For that to happen, first and foremost, you need to be willing to change. Every one of the following characteristics require that you have some degree of willingness to explore, do, learn, evaluate, try something that may be new or different, or do something you know how to do already but in a different way.

Additionally, you must be willing to change your book idea. The actual story, characters, subject, angle, theme, purpose, audience, or any number of other aspects of your project might need to be altered to make it viable in the marketplace. This may be difficult to swallow at first, but successful authorship relies on your ability to evaluate the marketability of your idea from every angle possible and to make the tough calls. Only when you have discovered that you have created a salable idea can you turn to writing the book. When you have completed the manuscript, you must be willing to receive feedback on how your writing and manuscript can be improved to make it successful and to make those changes.

Optimism. Whether you call it faith, positive thinking, reverse pessimism, Positive Psychology, or learned optimism, to become a successful author you must be willing to see everything that happens to you as pushing you closer to your goal of successful authorship. This means a rejection from an agent presents an opportunity to improve your query letter or your book proposal. A negative review of your manuscript by a book doctor at a conference presents a chance to rethink your plot or your content—or even to hone your craft. A session with a proposal consultant who tells you your platform section needs strengthening offers the opportunity to rethink your pre-promotion activity level.

Objectivity. To become a successful author you need to see yourself and your work objectively, from a different perspective than your own. Specifically, you need to see through the lens used by publishing professionals, such as literary agents and acquisitions editors. Both view your book idea not only as a creative project but also as a business proposition. They view you as a potential business partner. Even if you don't plan on seeking a traditional publisher for your book, you must learn to stand back and evaluate yourself and your work objectively from a publishing business perspective. Doing so becomes even more important if you plan to independently publish since you become the publisher of your own work.

The publishing industry is the book production and selling business; if you want to become an author you must be willing to make this your business as well. You have to be willing to craft your work with an eye to the industry's needs and standards, which are more often than not focused primarily on marketability and sales.

You also must distance yourself from your idea. You must detach from it so you are willing to receive, hear, and act upon criticism—and so you can learn to evaluate your idea and offer constructive criticism of your own. And you must make the necessary changes without cringing as if you are cutting off fingers and toes. You must do this with excitement because you know you are making the end product more salable. In other words, you must act in your book's best interest—even when it feels hard.

Ultimately, you must see your project from the perspective of the consumer, as well. Only when you do this can you pinpoint why they might pick up your book, carry it to the register, and purchase it, and then tell their friends they must read it, too. That's when you and your book become successful.

Tenacity. To become an author, you have to be willing to do whatever it takes for however long it takes to reach your goal. Determination, persistence, and perseverance carry you though to successful authorship, whether you are rewriting your manuscript, building author platform, submitting to the one hundredth agent, contacting the one thousandth reviewer, or writing the fiftieth blog post or press release about your book. You must have passion for your project and feel a sense of purpose. Every day you must show up eager to move forward, even if it is only by one small step or in spite of the challenges that have presented themselves.

You must love what you do. You must be in love with writing, being an author (or the prospect of becoming one), and your book. For you, authorship must not be about making money or selling books; writing books or this particular book must feel like a passion, a calling, a vocation, or a soul/sole purpose. This will keep you doing what must be done to succeed every day.

Despite this focus on Author Attitude, the need for a great idea and outstanding writing remain a factor in the success of any book. These will take you far. In all cases, to go the distance and become a successful author you need the elements included in an Author Attitude—Woot!

Completing Your Book in a Month

You can apply WOOT to your book-in-a-month challenge so you approach your project with the mindset and habits that help you achieve your goal. Here's how:

- **Willingness.** Be willing to take the challenge, adjust your schedule, ask for what you need, and make the necessary changes as the month unfolds. Be open to flow with challenges that come up during the month and to look for solutions.

- **Optimism.** Don't let yourself get mired down in pessimism when things don't go as planned. Remain optimistic about your ability to meet and overcome every obstacle—see it as an opportunity to move closer to your goal—and about your ability to do what you set out to do.

- **Objectivity.** Don't get too personally attached to your words. Remember that they will need to be edited. You are producing a first draft in a month, not necessarily a final draft. And write with your reader in mind; don't write for yourself. This will produce a better manuscript.

- **Tenacity.** Keep going! Do not give up. No excuses. This attitude will get you from Day 1 to Day 30. Persistence, determination, and perseverance will help you make it to the end of the book-in-a-month challenge.

And when you get to the end of Day 30, guess what? You will shout, "WOOT, WOOT!" And you will have great cause to celebrate. You will have written a book in a month. And you will have the attitude and skill to do it again . . . and again . . . and again.

ABOUT NINA AMIR

Nina Amir is an international speaker, award-winning blogger and journalist, 19X Amazon bestselling author, Author Coach, Transformational Coach, and one of 1,000 elite Certified High Performance Coaches in the world—the only one working with writers. Known as the Inspiration to Creation Coach, she helps people combine their purpose and passion, so they get inspired to action and Achieve More Inspired Results.

The author of *How to Blog a Book, The Author Training Manual, and Creative Visualization for Writers*, Amir also has authored 19 eBooks, including: *Authorpreneur: How to Build a Business Around Your Book, The Nonfiction Book Proposal Demystified,* and the *Write Nonfiction NOW!* series of six guides. She has had as many as six books on the same Amazon Top 100 list (Authorship) at the same time.

To further support writers, Nina founded the Nonfiction Writers' University, Write Nonfiction in November Challenge, and Author of Change Transformational Programs. She also created the Inspired Creator Community, which provides group Transformational (spiritual and personal growth) Coaching to nonfiction writers as well as non-writers. She also developed a proprietary author training program for aspiring authors and author coaches based on her book *The Author Training Manual* as well as a career planning program for writers, bloggers, and experts.

In 2015, Amir received a Certified High Performance Coach (CHPC') certification from the High Performance Institute, which was founded by New York Times bestselling author Brendon Burchard. She uses this to coach a variety of clients including writers.

Amir also offers personal development tools at NinaAmir.com and often teaches workshops, teleseminars, and webinars on how to become an author and achieve potential. She speaks to writing groups and at conferences internationally. She has been on the board of the BEA Bloggers event and the board of the National Association of Independent Writers and Editors.

Amir blogs at <u>How to Blog a Book</u>, <u>Write Nonfiction NOW!</u>, and <u>As the Spirit Moves Me</u>. She was a regular contributor to <u>theBookdesigner. com</u> and thefutureofink.com. She has also been the national Jewish Issue Examiner and the National Self-Improvement Examiner at Examiner.com and had a column on VibantNation.com.

Previously, Amir served as the writing and publishing expert on the popular <u>Dresser after Dark</u> radio show. For two years she was a featured expert on <u>Conversations with Mrs. Claus</u>, a podcast listened to by 130,000 people in 90 countries each month.

Amir earned a Bachelor of Arts degree in Magazine Journalism with a concentration in psychology from Syracuse University's S.I. Newhouse School of Public Communications. She has edited or written for more than 45 magazines, newspapers, e-zines, and newsletters and produced hundreds of articles in the process. She has interviewed such well-known figures as Usher, Deepak Chopra, Pete Seeger, and Michael Harner. Her essays have been published in five anthologies and appeared in numerous e-zines and Internet article directories. She also has produced hundreds of guest blog posts for well-known sites, and her work has appeared in such books as *Spiritual Pregnancy* and the fifth edition of *How to Write a Book Proposal.*

Amir also has a proven track record as a nonfiction book editor. One of her client's books, *Enlightened Leadership*, was self-published and then purchased and re-released verbatim by Simon & Schuster; it sold over 320,000 copies. Another, *Radical Forgiveness*, won the Writer's Digest Self-Published Book Award (Inspirational category), received a contract from William Morrow but remained self-published and went on to sell 115,000+ copies; much later Sounds True purchased the book.

Born and raised in New York, Amir has traveled extensively around the world. She resides in Placitas, NM, with her husband. It is her passion to help writers remove blocks to success, stay inspired and motivated, and achieve impact with their work.

NINAAMIR
INSPIRATION TO *Creation* COACH

To learn more about Nina and the courses, programs, and coaching she offers, visit www.ninaamir.com.

ABOUT THE AUTHORS

Jay Artale abandoned her corporate career to become a digital nomad and full-time writer. She's an avid blogger and a nonfiction author helping travel writers and travel bloggers achieve their self-publishing goals. Join her at Birds of a Feather Press where she shares tips, advice, and inspiration to writers with an independent spirit.

Roy Peter Clark has taught writing at the Poynter Institute in St. Petersburg, Florida, since 1979. He is the author of four recent books on writing and language, all published by Little, Brown: *Writing Tools, The Glamour of Grammar, Help! For Writers* and *How to Write Short: Word Craft for Fast Times*. His recent essay in the New York Times, "The Short Sentence as Gospel Truth," became the most emailed story in the paper. His essays on writing can be found at www.poynter.org. You can find him on Twitter @RoyPeterClark. He has been referred to as "America's writing coach."

Rachel Z. Cornell created ProNagger.com to help people get things done. ProNagger has fundamentally shifted the worlds of productivity and project completion by combining New School Nagging, evolutionary psychology and the process of creating. Cornell's personable nature and innovative methods make it easy to stay focused throughout the life of a project.

Kristen Eckstein is a highly sought-after publishing authority, multi best-selling author and award-winning international speaker who has started over 50 publishing companies and published over 170 books and e-books. In fall 2013 she challenged herself to write and published a new Kindle book every week for 18 weeks straight.

Denis Ledoux, author (Maine Writing Fellow 1991, 1996) and educator (B.A. English, M.A. Ed.), is director of the The Memoir Network (previously The Soleil Lifestory Network). He leads a team of coaches, editors, ghostwriters, and book producers that has helped tens of thousands of people to write their personal and family stories. His *Turning Memories Into Memoirs/A Handbook for Writing Lifestories* (1992, 1998, 2006) is classic in the memoir-writing field and, along with his many other titles, is available in both hardcopy and electronic forms.

Linda Joy Myers is president and founder of the National Association of Memoir Writers and a therapist for 35 years. Her memoir _Don't Call Me Mother: A Daughter's Journey from Abandonment to Forgiveness_ is a finalist in the ForeWord Book of the Year Award, a finalist in the IndieExcellence Awards, and received Honorable Mention in the New York Book Awards. She's also the author of three books on memoir writing: _The Power of Memoir—How to Write Your Healing Story_, _Journey of Memoir_, and _Becoming Whole_. Linda co-edited the anthology _Times They Were A-Changing—Women Remember the '60s & '70s_, a ForeWord Review Book of the Year finalist and IndieExcellence finalist. Her fiction, nonfiction, and memoir pieces have been published in literary journals and online. She writes for the Huffington Post, and co-teaches the program Write Your Memoir in Six Months. Linda is a speaker about memoir, healing, and the power of writing the truth, and offers editing, coaching, and manuscript evaluation for writers. www.namw. org. http://memoriesandmemoirs.com

Roger C. Parker is an experienced book coach and author who helps executives in transition learn from the examples of others, guiding them step-by-step through the process of planning, writing, promoting, and profiting from a published book.

Roger's first book, _Looking Good in Print_, was the first design book written for mainstream business readers, launching careers around the world. It ultimately sold over 350,000 copies, translated into over a dozen languages.

Since then, his 40+ books, including several in the ..._for Dummies_ series, has helped a generation of entrepreneurs and business professionals leverage the power of computer software and the Internet for career growth and mobility.

Along the way, Roger has interviewed over 500 A-list bestselling authors and marketers, helping him understand the DNA of profitable nonfiction book publishing.

Learn more at www.rogercparker.com and www.publishedandprofitable. com, or follow Roger on Twitter @rogercparker.

Lee Pound is a writing coach, book editor, publisher, and seminar producer. He is the author of *Profitable Social Media - Business Results Without Playing Games* and *57 Steps to Better Writing* and editor and co-author of *Coaching For The New Century*, *Adapt or Perish!*, and *Adapt! How to Survive and Thrive in the Changing World of Work*. He has also written three novels and several family histories.

Lee is a sought after speaker on writing and social media, edited award-winning weekly newspapers for 15 years, and has a deep knowledge of public and private companies from 20 years as a chief financial officer in the publishing industry. He is a partner in the CSL Writers Workshop and CSL Publishers. He was co-producer of the Speak Your Way to Wealth seminars, where he shared the stage with many powerful speakers. His clients write influential books in the fields of business, health, sales, and goal-setting. (www.leepound.com)

Ellen Violette is the CEO of Create a Splash LLC, a premier publishing, coaching, and online marketing company. She's also a #1 Best-selling author, a two-time eLit award-winner, a contributing writer to Published Magazine, & a recipient of the "Be the Change Award" as well as a highly-acclaimed copywriter.

Ellen specializes in helping independent professionals , speakers, and coaches create wealth the write way!

She is world-renown for her ground breaking 3 Days to E-Book Cash Workshop which has turned frustrated writers into successful and best-selling authors all over the world and for her digital publishing savvy, helping authors turn their books into best-sellers!

Ellen has been online since 2004 and been writing copy since 1997. She has a unique energetic style with no-hype and she gets results! She's also a Grammy-nominated songwriter and has a knack for helping authors find their own voice, get their message out to the world, and hopefully make it a better place!

Vicki C. Weiland has been a freelance writer and developmental editor/book doctor for over twenty-five years, specializing in fine arts, history, and business.

She is a former Board Member of <u>BAIPA</u> (Bay Area Independent Publishers Association) and <u>WNBA-SF</u> (Women's National Book Association, San Francisco). She has been a presenter and panelist at the San Francisco Writers Conference and the San Francisco Writing for Change Conference. She is currently launching "VCW Publishing" for e-Books, with subsequent hardback editions. This will include an amplification of her "Four Questions," which she hopes will be a further incentive for happy and productive writing—not only *in November* . . . but all year long! Contact: <u>vcweiland-writer@comcast.net</u>

ACKNOWLEDGEMENTS

The chapter that mentions "Author Attitude" is reprinted from _The Author Training Manual: A Comprehensive Guide to Writing Books that Sell_ by permission of Writer's Digest Books/Penguin Random House and the author. Copyright © 2014 Nina Amir.

Many of the chapters in this eBook first appeared on the Write Nonfiction NOW! blog and are reprinted in this book with permission.

MORE FROM NINA AMIR

The Write Nonfiction NOW! Guides

Write Nonfiction NOW! Guides are edited by Nina Amir, the founder of the Write Nonfiction in November Challenge, also know as NaNonFiWriMo (National Nonfiction Writing Month), and include tips from bestselling authors, seasoned writing coaches, and those who have successfully taken the Write Nonfiction in November Challenge. Each guide teaches a unique aspect of becoming a successful nonfiction author. These guides inform and motivate authors, businesspeople, and even non-writers to use their purpose and passion to create desirable and publishable products.

Click the following links to check out guides to:

- Writing and Publishing Articles
- Creativity and Flow
- Building Author Platform
- Virtual Book Tours
- A Writing Habit

To find more books by Nina Amir, go to www.booksbyninaamir.com.

The Nonfiction Writers' University

The Nonfiction Writers' University provides you with a comprehensive education you need to succeed as a nonfiction writer. Members receive the Author Training 101-104 course, a seven-year archive of interviews with writing and publishing experts, eBook writing guides, courses, and monthly group Author Coaching sessions, during which you can get your questions answered and receive support on challenges you encounter on the path to nonfiction authorship.

The Inspired Creator Community

The Inspired Creator Community offers a personal and spiritual growth curriculum and group coaching program based in esoteric wisdom, Certified High Performance Coaching and Transformational Coaching for those who want to learn how create what matters to them in a spiritually guided manner. Members learn to be the type of people who have the mindsets and habits that allow them to create change from the inside out and live lives that feed their souls.

Inspired
CREATOR / COMMUNITY

Made in the USA
Las Vegas, NV
27 December 2024

15465237R00109